Quakers in Plymouth

A Friends' Meeting in context 1654 to the 1960's

Martin Wyatt

.

ISBN 978-1-904446-92-7

Published and printed by
Quacks Books
7 Grape Lane
Petergate
York YO1 7HU

Contents

Quakers in Plymouth

A Friends' Meeting in context 1654 to the 1960's

Introduction

Quakers have from time to time made a notable contribution to Plymouth life, either individually or corporately, and those contributions were usually well recognised at the time. They constitute one theme of this history. Another theme is the part played by Plymouth in the Quaker life of the West Country. That Plymouth was for 300 years by far the largest Meeting in Devon and Cornwall did not mean that it dominated; but it did play a vital part in ensuring that Quakerism not only survived but flourished, particularly in west Devon. Two subsidiary themes are the continual tendency of Plymouth Friends to fiddle about with land and buildings, and, from the end of the 18th century, their interest and activity in education.

The history of a Quaker Meeting should be in part a segment of the history of where it is located, in part a segment of the wider history of Quakers, and in part an account of the interactions between a group of individuals. A local Quaker history can be neither restrictedly local nor exclusively Quaker. I have tried to write the story of an ever-changing group of people I hope it will give you some idea of what that group achieved, what can be said about being a member of it, and how it changed. In trying to evoke the life of the past, I have aimed to include what was significant, some examples of what was typical, but also what I found amusing.

The focus on the Meeting means that less attention is paid to individual Friends than some might expect. Nevertheless, certain individuals and families figure more largely than others, partly because of the greater contribution that they made, and consequently the greater amount of information available on them, and partly because of my attempts to dig out the origins of significant developments. A little more about leading individuals will be found in the notes.

I do not believe it possible to be an impartial historian or reporter – the narration may be strictly factual, but selection is unavoidable, and selection depends on individual judgment. So although I believe everything that follows is properly supported by the records, I think the reader should know the writer's basic views. I am a Quaker, and have been a great admirer of the boldness and directness of the early Friends. I have also admired the energy and devotion of the evangelical Friends of the 19th century, but I have never responded to the beliefs they expounded.

The records available are abundant but can be frustrating. Sometimes major decisions were taken by small groups of men (sic), and only recorded afterwards if at all, so that key information is lacking. There are continuous runs of minute books for Quarterly, Monthly, and Preparative Meetings almost from their origins (a bit later in the case of the Women's Monthly Meeting). There are other minute books, though some are missing, and there are deeds, a few letters and other papers and some plans, but a shortage of anything more personal to bring to life the formal records. A special case is the period from 1654 to 1685 when the propagandist writings of the early Quakers and their recording of sufferings more than compensate for the scantiness and erratic nature of the minutes. The materials become more ample with the passage of time, but I have tried to keep a balance between the centuries. Obvious non-Quaker sources have also been used. I do not pretend to have read everything I could have read. To scan through all the minutes written during 300 years of meetings for discipline is no proper occupation for human beings; yet smothered in the dust of the formulaic repetitions are occasional vivid glimpses of life at the time. Some of these have been thrown up by my stirring through the dust when searching for something else. There are doubtless others I have not found. I have particularly searched for the origins of new developments, with varying success. The notes provide the necessary references and also some additional information.

Spelling and punctuation have been been modernised throughout, but the use of capitals varies. The Quaker system of dating, explained in the notes, has mostly been maintained, for as long as it was used. A glossary is provided.

In writing this history, I have from time to time thought of the words of an 18th century American Quaker, John Woolman: "As looking over the minutes made by persons who have put off this body hath sometimes revived in me a thought how ages pass away; so this list [of members] may probably revive a like thought when I, and the rest of the persons above-named, are centred in another state of being."

M W

Acknowledgements

In writing this history, I have necessarily accumulated debts of gratitude. First among them is to the late Douglas Selleck, whose various writings on Plymouth Quakers have provided leads and information, though I have found a couple of errors in his work, and have often disagreed with his selection or interpretation of material. He made no real attempt to give an account of Plymouth Friends after the 18th century.

I am grateful to Rosemary Moore, who provided expert comment on the first two chapters of his history, and to James Gregory of Plymouth University, who generously responded to a request from a complete stranger to comment very helpfully on the fourth chapter. Three Friends from Plymouth Meeting, John Eales, Manfred Kemmner and Rosalie Wyatt have read drafts of each chapter as they have appeared. All have made improvements and saved me from mistakes. Remaining errors are my own.

Staff at Friends House Library, the Plymouth and West Devon Record Office, and Plymouth City Council Library have always been helpful, sometimes exceptionally so. I have also used the library of the Plymouth Athenaeum and the Plymouth Quaker library. John Lawson and Toby Bainton have kindly provided additional information.

Photographs of Treville Street Meeting House, Adult School, and burial ground are reproduced by permission of Devon Area Meeting of the Religious Society of Friends. Aerial photo of the north end of Mutley Plain courtesy of Chris Robinson. The cover picture is reproduced by permission of Plymouth Meeting. I am grateful to the Sessions Book Trust for their contribution to the printing costs.

MW

Chapter 1

The Beginnings

Quaker preachers first came into Plymouth in the summer of 1654. At that time Plymouth was a thriving commercial town with a population probably of around 8,000. It was also definitely a puritan town, the only Parliamentary stronghold in the West Country, to hold out against Royalist forces during the Civil War. Its dominant form of puritanism was presbyterian, with fixed Calvinistic beliefs and definitely supporting the role of the clergy and the existing social hierarchies. There were others who thought differently, and the Baptists had been present for some time, recently establishing a chapel. The Civil War was some six years in the past, but the country had not settled down into a stable form of government. Oliver Cromwell had been installed as Lord Protector in the previous year and was ruling basically with the support of the Army. Cromwell's instincts were mainly in favour of toleration of different sects, but the way in which national policy was implemented depended very much on the great people locally. Among these in Plymouth, the Mayor, who was the chief magistrate, was the most significant, though changing each year in September.

The new preachers who had arrived were subversive, both religiously and socially. They were religiously subversive because they told people that they did not need a hireling clergy but should rely on their own inward light, and, even worse, that it was possible to be without sin – views that they had no inhibitions about expressing. They were socially subversive because they treated everyone as equal: they would not take their hats off to anyone, and they addressed a social superior as "thou" or "thee" when it was accepted that one should use the plural "you" to people of a higher standing. This was a class-defined society, in which a person's social position was

1

meticulously recorded in legal documents.

The two Quakers who arrived in 1654 were John Audland, well known in early Quaker history, and Thomas Airey. They were part of a particular movement at this time to send out travelling ministers, usually in pairs. This movement had started in the north of England, and Audland and Airey were both from Westmorland. Quakerism had not appeared from nowhere. In different parts of the country there had been half-organised groups of people with the same sort of religious experience, Plymouth probably among them. But now there was a movement.

The way of going about this evangelising work was already well-established. Either beforehand or on arrival the travelling ministers[1] would make enquiries about groups or individuals who were likely to be sympathetic to their message. Presumably this was the case in Plymouth, because it was reported that they were received "of many who were waiting for the Lord's appearance", indicating that there had already been some people in Plymouth with the same sort of thinking and experiences. However, following up such contacts was not all they did. They "stayed . . . about 4 or 5 days, and had several Meetings . . both public & private, & on the first day (First Day meaning Sunday[2]) the said John Audland went to one of the Steeple houses in this town" (this probably meaning St Andrew's church, as Charles Church had not yet been completed at that time), "& testified against the priest & their worship, & also sounded Truth amongst them, for which the said John Audland received from the people in the Steeple house pretty much abuse ; and the said Thomas Airey, he went to the Baptist Meeting, & sounded truth amongst them, who stood in great opposition to his testimony."[3] Although some people were convinced, these travelling ministers did not establish a Quaker Meeting.

In March 1655 two other travelling minsters, Thomas Salthouse and Miles Hallhead, both of them also from north-west England, together with a Friend from Bristol, Nicholas Ganncliffe, arrived to carry on the work. Audland and Airey had been and gone, but the Plymouth Quakers later testified that Salthouse and Hallhead first gathered them into a Meeting, and that their staunchness under persecution helped to confirm the new converts.[4] They had several peaceable meetings, at which many were "turned from darkness to light". These culminated in a meeting at the house of John Harris, on the edge of the town on the way to Stonehouse. This was so large that it had to move into the garden, and there "did they declare the truth of the experience of what they had found of the free grace of God." The account they gave of this meeting emphasised, firstly, that they spoke of their own religious experience, and secondly that they spoke in plainness and simplicity, "without using any inveighing against men or opinions." The chaplain of a naval frigate, George Brookes, spoke in praise of what they had said, but he was probably antagonised by Thomas Salthouse asking him whether he lived the life of what he spake, and also saying, in a general sort of way, that the one who enters the sheepfold not by the door is a thief. Nicholas Ganncliffe took issue with Brookes's talking about a Trinity in Unity and a Unity in Trinity. [5]

There are two conflicting accounts of what happened after this. Hallhead and Salthouse said that they were taken out of a meeting at Robert Cary's house and taken before the Mayor, John Paige. They were imprisoned without charge, and examined in private the next day. However, Henry Hatsell, who was the naval agent at Plymouth, and also a justice of the peace, wrote to the Secretary of the Admiralty on 25 May 1655: "Here came to this place, about five days since, three quakers from Bristol, and the last Lord's Day they gathered people together in house at the outskirt of this Corporation, and there they made discoveries of new lights. And two days since they heard that the Mayor would send for them. Came to him with . . . "what wilt thou have of us?" and with their hats on, which much amazed the people." The Quaker from Bristol was discharged, and "the other two are committed [to imprisonment], where they have been two

3

days, and, as an honest man told me just now, since they have been in prison they have neither sought God by prayer nor craved a blessing on what they have received, nor returned thanks." He added in a postscript, "The Quakers are still in prison being very stiff and are like to be sent to the Common Gaol, our quiet west country people do judge them to be men of a strange humour." [6]

The Mayor, being asked why their imprisonment was continued, said that it was for denying the Trinity. They wrote a letter explaining their position and when the enquiry was repeated, the Mayor said that they would not take the oath abjuring the Pope. As Quakers would not take any oaths (which implied a double standard of truth), this was a fairly common way of dealing with them. They were sent to Exeter and imprisoned there, despite Robert Cary and Arthur Cotton offering to enter into a recognisance for their appearance at the Assize.

In the same year, 1655, George Fox came to Plymouth and "had a very precious meeting" in Robert Cary's house, but he was not mentioned by Plymouth Quakers in the account of their origins. Instead they wrote about Margaret Killam (or Killin) and Barbara Pattison. Margaret Killam was a member of an important Quaker group centred on Balby in South Yorkshire. This group had originated before George Fox came and preached in the area. She herself had already preached in other parts of the country including Cambridge and Reading. Barbara Pattison was also from the north of England. Presumably the mention by Plymouth Friends means that these two travelling ministers were active in providing support, but we only know that Margaret Killam spoke in private to the Mayor, who by then was Christopher Ceely, and that Barbara Pattison interrupted a funeral. Note that at this time women were not expected to give religious instruction in public, let alone to a local dignitary. Quakers were among the first to recognise women's religious equality. Margaret Killam was accompanied by Margaret Dyer, wife of Edward Dyer, and the Mayor admitted that what she said was very good, but nonetheless shut her up in a cold room (this was December) and

4

when local Friends came asking about her, he threw an elderly woman down the stairs with his own hands. He sent Margaret Killam off to Exeter with her legs tied under the horse. There she was held on various pretexts and eventually released. Barbara Pattison spoke to a priest, Thomas Martin, while he was preaching a funeral sermon. This was a definite offence against a law of Queen Mary's reign, and she was regularly tried and imprisoned for three months.[7] Together, Killam and Pattison published a pamphlet, published in London: *A warning from the Lord to the teachers & people of Plimovth. With a few queries to the parish teachers of this nation, that have great sums of money for teaching the people. From them which are scornfully called Qvakers, but witness the teaching of Christ.* In this they said, "Thus saith the Lord, I have sent my sons and daughters from far, I have raised up prophets among you . . . but some of my messengers you have imprisoned, and others you have evil entreated."[8] Margaret Killam seems to have returned home, but Barbara Pattison is later mentioned as being in Cornwall.[9]

Two Quaker women from Plymouth also ended up imprisoned at Exeter about this time. Priscilla Cotton (or Cotten) and Mary Cole went in August 1656 to the steeplehouse, where they sat silent till George Hughes the priest had ended what they called his divination. Priscilla Cotton then stood up and said, "People, why do you spend your money for that which is not bread, and your labour for that which doth not satisfy? Hearken diligently to the eternal word, that your souls may live." She had an altercation with the priest, who called on the magistrates, despite the fact that what had been done was not illegal because she had waited till the service was over. Thereupon Mary Cole said, "Did ever Jesus Christ or his Apostles call for the assistance of magistrates?" The magistrates (who would have been in the congregation) tendered the oath for the abjuration of the Pope, which of course the Quakers refused to take, though they did renounce the Pope. They were imprisoned at Exeter till the next Assize, when they were freed because no evidence appeared. While they were in prison they wrote a pamphlet *To the Priests and People of England,* justifying women's preaching, and this seems to have been approved by the Quaker leadership.[10]

Hallhead and Salthouse, meanwhile had been fined £5, apparently on the grounds that they had wronged George Brookes and refused to take the oath abjuring the Pope, and were imprisoned until it was paid. They were, however, released in 1657.[11] Salthouse continued to visit Devon and Cornwall, and eventually settled at St Austell (which the Quakers called Austell).[12] He is occasionally listed as attending the Friends' Devon Quarterly Meeting and the Plymouth Monthly Meeting.

The names and standing of quite a few Plymouth Quakers at this time have been preserved for us by various means. In Plymouth as elsewhere in the country, the Quakers appealed mainly to the middling sort. There were very few gentry among them. Despite his belief in equality before God, George Fox thought it worth mentioning that Elizabeth Trevelyan, a baronet's daughter, was among those he met at Plymouth. Nor were there many labourers. The people who were convinced were small farmers, merchants and suchlike. These were people who were accustomed to think for themselves. In Plymouth some quite substantial citizens joined the movement, and often their servants did also.

It seems likely that within a few years of first coming together, Plymouth Quakers were meeting in a house on the Hoe, while renting a burial ground adjacent to it. These are thought to have been in the vicinity of the present Sussex Street. In 1860 when new houses were being built on the site, human remains were discovered, and these were transferred to the burial ground behind the Treville Street meeting house.[13] There is little information on the life of the Meeting. To judge by later evidence, there would have been two or three meetings a week, but only one on each day. The meetings might have been of any length.

The evidence from the 1670s also shows that in Devon the pattern

6

of Quaker meetings kept on changing, and it seems likely that this had been happening earlier, with new meetings appearing and others disappearing. Plymouth and Kingsbridge, however, seem to have been constant.

In February 1660 one of the travelling ministers, Alexander Parker, reported that "We are come to Plymouth this day & had a very large meeting of precious friends – all is quiet to us and our friends at present." In September of the same year, a Plymouth Quaker, Priscilla Cotton, reported: "The priests are much shattered & the Baptists are much shattered & there is an inclination in the people after truth and since dear Thomas Salthouse came last among us he hath been very serviceable in riding up and down amongst Friends at their meetings, and friends have been refreshed and strengthened & verily I see a necessity for his abiding in these parts some time for there is need both in Cornwall and Devonshire. Meetings have been pretty large & some Baptists and others have come to meetings & one Baptist lately convinced of the Truth amongst us who said he never heard the truth in all his life before he heard Thomas Salthouse declare among us, though he be old in years . . . . We enjoy our meetings peaceably & the wicked is much chained down at present."[14]

This, however, was the high point for the early Plymouth Quakers. 1660 was the year in which the monarchy was restored, and a wave of anti-republican sentiment led to the election of the "Cavalier Parliament", whose members were determined to restore the Church of England as the only church in the country. Among many others, the Quakers' former persecutors Christopher Ceely and William Yeo were removed from office as magistrate and Town Clerk respectively because they remained true to their old beliefs in refusing to take the oaths of allegiance and supremacy, which recognised the king as the head of the church. The Quakers were to attract new and more systematic persecution.

Chapter 2

Organisation and persecution

In 1661 the Fifth Monarchist uprising in London prompted a new level of persecution of all suspicious groups, Quakers among them, although the Quaker leadership had published its first declaration of pacifism. In 1662 the Quaker Act was passed, targeting the Quaker refusal to take oaths and also their holding of meetings. It was strengthened by the Conventicle Act of 1664.

Even before the Quaker Act was passed, in January 1661, nine named Quakers were imprisoned at Exeter for refusing to take oaths. And on the first proclamation banning Quaker meetings and requiring justices of the peace to administer the oath of allegiance, the Exeter prisons of the High Gaol and Bridewell were thronged with over 70 Quakers, "among whom were all the Men Inhabitants of that persuasion in Plymouth." This might not mean all the men in the Meeting, as there were some from outside the town; but we are told that the women kept up the Meetings. The Mayor sent for them and asked why they met contrary to the King's command. They replied that it was in discharge of their duty to God. The Mayor sent them away with threats. There is no account of how the men got out of prison, but by August there were male Friends at a meeting in Plymouth which was broken up by soldiers, some being brought to the Mayor and imprisoned at Exeter. The same happened in September.[1]

One reason we know about these events is that the Quaker leadership was insistent that Friends should record their sufferings and send them to London. In difficult times this may not have been done consistently, or alternatively the persecution was spasmodic, because the next accounts are from October 1663, when eight men and one woman were fined for non-attendance at church; April 1665, when 18 men were committed to prison for non-payment of a fine; August 1666, when 15 men were committed to prison for non-payment of a fine; and May 1670 when 14 men had goods distrained.[2]

A more positive view of the Meeting comes from the knowledge that in 1666 Plymouth Friends were taking fresh supplies to a ship in the Sound, the *Black Eagle*. This was carrying London Quakers whom the authorities were trying to transport to Barbados.[3]

In 1669 the amount of information we have on Plymouth Quakers increases. George Fox had been going round the country, systematising what he called Quarterly Meetings (that is, meetings of senior Friends meeting once a quarter), mostly based on counties, and adding Monthly Meetings and women's meetings alongside them. All these were meetings to deal with worldly affairs and church discipline. A Quarterly Meeting covered a larger area and took all the major decisions. In our case it covered Devon, and was called interchangeably either the Quarterly Meeting or the County Meeting. The Monthly Meetings typically contained one to three "particular" meetings, in our case either Plymouth and Kingsbridge, or Plymouth on its own. They dealt with local arrangements, lapses, marriages, and minor disciplinary matters and disputes. Difficult matters were usually referred to the Quarterly Meeting, but this sometimes referred them back again, saying they should settle it themselves. The Men's Meeting was always called **the** Monthly or Quarterly Meeting, but there was also a parallel Women's Meeting, with different functions. These were select gatherings, not open to everyone. It is not clear how the first members of the Monthly Meeting were chosen, but once chosen they became a self-selecting group. As the meetings took place at times when most men were at work, only the most prosperous could participate. The Quarterly Meeting was made up of Monthly Meeting representatives.

Now, these meetings kept minutes.

The earliest minute book we have in Plymouth starts in 1669, and is for an unnamed Monthly Meeting which covered Plymouth and Kingsbridge to begin with, and then, from 1676, just Plymouth. The writing is difficult to read in places. It is written in dark brown ink on light brown paper, and the scribe tended to start off writing carefully and then degenerate; he crammed lines together so that symbols overlap (this is the worst aspect), and he deleted words with a sort of spiral motion which could go anywhere.

The first minute is about a collection which had been ordered by the Quarterly Meeting. There are four other minutes from that meeting, one of which deals with a dispute with Mary and Nicholas Cole. This dispute dragged on. Mainly it was about Mary Cole not coming to meeting, and having dealings with a priest. Both Mary and Nicholas had been prominent in the early days of the meeting. As we have seen, Mary went with Priscilla Cotton to speak in church, and both were imprisoned. Nicholas was one of the nine Quakers imprisoned in January 1661 for refusing to take oaths. The dispute dragged on.

John Light, a prosperous clothier, was always named the first in attendance lists, and his contributions to collections were the largest, often twice the amount of the next donor. Arthur Cotton was also prominent. When the leadership in London arranged a meeting of county representatives, it was the Plymouth Friends who were asked to appoint the representative from Devon. Early on, there is a rota for two Friends to attend the Quarterly, or County Meeting each quarter, but later the representatives are appointed just before the Quarterly Meeting. The so-called Monthly Meetings were by no means monthly, which is not surprising given the difficulties, or, if they were, there were meetings when nothing was recorded in the book.

Because the minute book deals largely in disciplinary matters, it

11

probably gives a distorted view of what was happening. In 1671/2, it was reported that Mary Cole had been visited by Friends from the Men's Meeting, and also two Women Friends from the Women's Meeting, so that clearly there was also a Women's Monthly Meeting, though no minute book has survived.[4] As time passed, there were also minutes about other Friends who did not come to meeting, and answers in writing were often requested. We do not know whether these Friends who did not attend were simply falling away, possibly under the pressure of the persistent persecution. It would be understandable if not everyone had a faith strong enough to enable them to go repeatedly into the crowded and repulsive conditions of a seventeenth century gaol, however much they might be sustained by their fellow Quakers. Alternatively these non-attenders may have been influenced by a new tendency among some Quakers at about this time, asserting that it was wrong to have fixed times and places for coming together in worship, which should happen only when so moved by the Spirit.

National events were probably impacting on the local situation in ways we cannot know. In 1672 Charles II issued a Declaration of Indulgence, suspending the penal laws against nonconformists and Roman Catholics. In the following year, however, he was obliged to recall Parliament, and Parliament in turn obliged him to revoke the Declaration. It is likely that there was still no strong enforcement of the laws until 1675, when the king issued an order for the penal laws to be strictly enforced. During this period of comparative calm, the Quakers acquired their first permanent meeting house.

The lease of two buildings in Bilbury Street was acquired on 4 March 1674 in the name of John Light, probably bought from someone called Ambrose Hind. Old maps appear to show that at this time streets did not have definitive names. In older documents the location is always referred to as Bilbury Street, but later it was referred to as Treville Street. In between, it seems to have been labelled Lower Broad Street, or even, in a newspaper report of

1812, just Broad Street. It was in the area of Bretonside – towards the north of the town as it then was, and just south of the newly built Charles Church. The roundabout which goes round Charles Church now goes through part of what was the Quaker burial ground at the back of the building. The Lessors were John Beare junior, Alice his wife (daughter of Ambrose Hind) and George Beare, all of Bearscombe, near Kingsbridge. John and George Beare may have been the grandsons of the John Beare who was a notorious persecutor of nonconformists. The lease was granted for 99 years, but to end on the death of the survivor of three persons. These were Nicholas Harris, son of John Harris of Pennycross, yeoman; Patience, the daughter of Francis Light, house carpenter; and Mary, daughter of John Croker of Plymouth, gentleman. These leases on three lives were common in Devon at the time, and were frequently renewed on the third death. The list of names gives some idea of the mix of Friends in Plymouth meeting at the time.

This site was to provide a home for Plymouth Friends for well over 200 years, though their undisturbed occupation of it lasted only three years to begin with.

A fund was raised for adapting the buildings, and we have a record of who paid how much out of the £373.13s.06d. The adaptations meant that parts of the buildings could still be used for residential use, as there were tenants, who later gave rise to concern about their disorderly behaviour and had to be given notice. In 1678 a Quaker, Katharine Martindale was allowed to live there rent free, subject to conditions. In May 1681 John Light, who had made the biggest contribution to the work on the building, was still owed £8 on it, but this was immediately paid off. Now, and well into the 19th century, Friends in the position of a treasurer (whether or not they were called that) made the disbursements for the Meeting even if they had not received the income to cover it, and frequently ended up being owed money, which then had to be paid off. [5]

13

Concerning the first burial ground, on the Hoe, rented before the first meeting house was acquired, in1674 it was ". . . unanimously concluded, that none whatsoever shall be buried in our burying place but such who are faithful friends .... & with which friends have unity."[6]

In July 1676 the Monthly Meeting set down the form for a certificate of marriage, probably on a national model. The man and woman marrying both made the same declaration, but may have been able to add to the wording as they were moved. The Monthly Meeting also had to approve marriages, and in this it went about its task very carefully, particularly to ensure that the two parties did not have any commitment to anyone else. The first procedural decision, made in October 1677, was that the two parties should first get the approval of the women's monthly meeting, and this should send representatives to the men's meeting, where the final decision would be made. The procedure was not always adhered to, and the question was often put off to the next meeting. This clearly caused some distress, so an attempt was made to ensure that it could be dealt with at the first meeting it came to, but it was not long before it was again normal for it to be deferred.

In the midst of all the persecution and the getting organised, Friends still found time to fall out with each other. In 1674 there is a paper, signed by six Friends, setting out 16 Articles of dispute between Matthew Crooker and Richard Browne of Lyneham, and giving the decision on each of them. The disputes were mainly about nasty things that Richard Browne was alleged to have said about Matthew Crooker, but one of them was about a maidservant whom Matthew Crooker had taken from Richard Browne, with his consent. She had then returned to her former master, who refused to give her back. All the decisions went against Richard Browne, and in some cases he admitted that he had been wrong, or would have been wrong if he had said what was attributed to him. It seems that the maidservant had no say in what happened. At the end, the paper urges that "from henceforwards you would not let or suffer any root of bitterness to take place & grow in you. . ."[7] It says something for these early Friends that the admonition seems to have been acted upon. Richard Browne continued to be in fairly good standing, as he was given a paid job by the Quarterly Meeting. In 1680 however, he was in trouble for having given recognisance for his appearance at the Assizes (presumably he should have maintained that his word was good enough, and let himself be imprisoned). Later on, Matthew Crooker was admonished for backsliding, and then had a dispute with someone else, in which he was adjudged to be in the wrong, but the dispute did not prevent his being in good standing.[8]

We know about Richard Browne's appointment to the paid job, and get a look at the wider picture in Devon because there is a Devon Quarterly Meeting minute book starting in 1676, though we know that Quarterly Meetings were held before then. In this the first minute is about arranging for Richard Browne "of Lynon" (Lyneham) to "transcribe all such Papers as doe come abroad for the Service of Friends of this County" and payment for his labour and charge. Clearly, this was the method of disseminating instructions and exhortations from the central leadership. For communications with the leadership, Arthur Cotton of Plymouth seems to have been the correspondent. We know that he wrote to George Fox, and later on the Quarterly Meeting appointed him to gather up the reports of sufferings to send in.[9]

The minute book shows that Quarterly Meetings were held regularly, though there are several meetings where nothing is recorded except the date of the next meeting. In two of the years the spring meeting is appointed for "The 5th day in the Assize week". This minute book, the Women's Quarterly Meeting minute book and the Plymouth and Kingsbridge minute book contain various lists of the Monthly and particular Meetings in Devon dating from different times. When these are compared, it is clear that Meetings came and went in other parts of the county. Plymouth and Kingsbridge seem to be comparatively stable compared with what was going on elsewhere, and we have already seen Plymouth's importance as the meeting which would send a county representative to London when one was needed.

In the same year, 1676, Nicholas Cole died. The grounds of his dispute with Plymouth Friends were never fully recorded in the minute books, but there seem to have been two elements. One was that he persisted in defending his wife in her talking to a priest and her not coming to Meeting. The other was that he had unauthorised correspondence with London. These two elements may or may not have been related. At his death it was recorded that he had turned aside from the truth and separated himself from Friends.[10]

From 1676, although nothing is said about it, there is no record of Monthly Meetings being held at Kingsbridge as well as Plymouth, though in 1678 the meeting dealt with a forged certificate said to have been sent from Kingsbridge Friends to Bristol. These certificates were commonly issued to Friends moving elsewhere to state that they were in good standing with the Meeting they came from. In this case the certificate for a father and son, Richard Marsh the elder and the younger, was disowned.[11]

In 1675 persecution had been resumed again, with a particularly severe outbreak in 1677. On 5 April, Andrew Horseman, the Mayor, dispersed the meeting and fined Richard Samble £20 for preaching. On 7 April, the Sunday, he came again, haled them into the street, set a guard on the door, and fined Richard Samble another £40 for preaching. Another account adds that Richard Samble had been on his knees in prayer, and that the fine was laid on four persons. They were kept out of the Meeting House till 29 September, when William Toms took office as Mayor. Afterwards the new Mayor followed the example of his predecessor and kept them out. They assembled in the street three times a week, enduring the cold and inclemency of the weather, for over 12 months, "abused by the rabble and scum of the people, and sometimes by the officers and soldiers of the garrison, who threw squibs of fire and hot burning coals upon them, pushing them up and down the street, and bedaubing them with filthy excrements." [12] Presumably as a result of this, in July of 1677, all men Friends were desired to be at the next Monthly Meeting, instead of the select few who normally came.

The Women's Quarterly Meeting minute book dates from 1681, which is when the women first started holding Quarterly Meetings. On being commissioned to acquire a book for the minutes, women Friends of Cullompton went out and purchased quite a large book, into which the first entries had been carefully copied, in a clear round hand, well spaced. On the whole the women had much better writing than the men. In several subsequent meetings, there is much about a woman Friend who got married by a priest, and does not know she has done any evil. There seems to have been considerable forbearance due to pleading by her sister. Another Friend walking disorderly was given shorter shrift, and a testimony given against her. In both cases, the women's meeting seems to have taken the initiative and largely dealt with it, but brought in the men's meeting to finalise the action. After a few meetings, attendance falls, and the records are largely accounts of money raised for Quakers in need, with records of how they were allocated, and complaints about non-attendance at the meetings. Collections are sometimes said to be from named meetings, sometimes said to be raised at this QM, very occasionally given as from a named man, with none from a named woman. To begin with, all the disbursements were to women.

Persecution continued. In 1683, Walter Phillips wrote to Thomas Salthouse giving a list of 72 Friends in various prisons in Exeter, at least seven of whom were recognisably from Plymouth. [13] The records of the Meeting for Sufferings for 1684/5 show that John Light was a prisoner in one of the Exeter gaols, and at the same time was the correspondent providing the names of Quaker prisoners in those gaols. He later provided the same information writing from

Plymouth.

In 1685 James II came to the throne. The Quakers had good reason to think he would be favourable towards them, and presented him with a petition showing the number of Quakers in prison in each county. There were 104 in Devon, more than any other county except Yorkshire, which was much larger, though Devon was almost equalled by Bristol, which the Quakers counted separately because of its significance to them. In the same petition it was said that Plymouth's Quaker serge-makers would have kept above 500 poor people in work if they had not been imprisoned.[14] James issued a proclamation for a general pardon, and prisoners for religion were released and allowed to hold their meetings without much molestation.

It is worth noting that in 1686 several families of Plymouth Friends, with considerable numbers of servants emigrated to the new Quaker colony of Pennsylvania in America.[15] Yet the Meeting must have been thriving because in the same year, it was agreed to hold two Meetings on First Day (i.e. Sunday) and at this time the Monthly Meeting was approving one or two marriages a year. In 1689 a certificate was provided to Philadelphia for Francis Rawle, who had emigrated there, showing that he had no marriage commitments.[16]

In 1688 occurred the Glorious Revolution, as most Protestants called it, with William of Orange landing in Torbay; and in 1689 there was the Toleration Act. This put an end to serious persecution. In 1696 there was an Affirmation Act, making it unnecessary to swear oaths, though the wording of this was not settled to the satisfaction of all until 1722. After this it was no longer possible to get the better of Quakers simply because they would not swear oaths in court. From then on, the only serious problem for the Friends was their refusal to pay tithes, church rates, and war-related levies (see the next chapter). As only a few of them remained as farmers, and the collection of tithes in towns had been virtually abandoned, tithes were not a major issue for most of them, and the levies only lasted a comparatively short time.

The other event at this time that slowly came to affect the Plymouth Quakers was that William III established a major naval base and dockyard at Plymouth Dock, leading to the development of a new town on Plymouth's doorstep and a change in the character of its port. Neither Dock, later known as Devonport, nor the small town of Stonehouse was within the Plymouth municipal boundary until in 1914 the three towns, as they were called, were combined. Nevertheless the one Quaker Meeting covered all of them.

Chapter 3

The Eighteenth Century

The Quakers settled down to become a solid respectable sect, with their own peculiarities. The life that they led was shaped by outward constraints, by their beliefs, and by the way that their organisation worked.

One of the main outward constraints was that the Toleration Act only did what it said in its title, it tolerated, it did not enable. Specifically, it did not enable dissenters to take part in civic life, nor were they able to go to English universities (though a few did go to Scottish or foreign universities). Quaker energies were therefore put into other activities, and the more active Quakers made their mark in commerce, invention, the application of invention, and science.

Their beliefs, particularly those on equality and simplicity, continued to mark them out. Because they had an insistence on plain clothing, they had evolved a sort of uniform which was practical in many ways, but distinctive, as they did not follow the fashions of the times. They retained the practice of addressing others as thou or thee, long after it had ceased to be a social statement, and had become just an oddity. They did not use names for the months and days of the week, but numbers instead. These distinctions set them aside and made them easily recognisable. Their beliefs helped them to become a nurturing community, helping one another out, but also a fairly judgemental community. There is every indication that the conduct of the meeting for worship in Plymouth followed the same pattern as elsewhere. The elders and ministers, including any travelling ministers, would sit on a bench, probably a raised bench, facing the others. Both the elders' bench and those for the members would be divided by gender. The meeting would be held in silence until someone spoke, and this could be anyone, minister or not, and could be a message or a prayer, after which the silence would resume. If any travelling ministers were present, there would be an expectation that they would speak. This pattern and the arrangement of the meeting room continued into the 20th century, when the arrangement of the room altered.

This chapter deals first with the Meeting's wider connections, then with its business side, and how the approach to business worked out in the lives of William and Jacob Cookworthy. It then considers some disciplinary cases, and, by contrast, looks at Plymouth Friends' relationship with the life of the town. There is an account of some developments towards the end of the 18th century, and finally a brief look at the development of Quaker beliefs.

Plymouth Quakers maintained a sense of belonging to a wider movement. Most immediately this applied to the Devon Quarterly Meeting, which moved around various locations, the furthest from Plymouth being Cullompton, always with the possibility of bad weather and the usual difficulties of getting around in Devon at that time. On one occasion when Plymouth Friends were chided for not sending a representative to Exeter in winter, their reply was indignant, pointing out the problems of going nearly a hundred miles "when the days are short and the roads at the worst."[1]

Devon Quarterly Meeting would in turn be in touch with the Meeting for Sufferings which had by now progressed from just trying to deal with Friends' "sufferings" to becoming the central body dealing with national affairs in between meetings of the Yearly Meeting. Rather than sending representatives to this, the Quarterly Meetings were allocated correspondents from among the Meeting for Sufferings members, who were all London-based.

As part of the wider movement, local Friends would be offering hospitality to the travelling ministers who came among them. In 1693, the Monthly Meeting set up a rota of Friends to accompany such ministers on the next stage of their journey, and this was later renewed. In 1739 the Monthly Meeting recorded that their funds had been used to buy a horse, saddle etc for a travelling minister from New England – presumably he had landed at Plymouth – the money to be repaid on the return of the minister, when all this was sold, "if the horse lives till then".[2]

Plymouth's Quaker ministers also travelled around. Around the end of the century, Sarah Abbott went as far as Ireland, where she was "at times brought under close exercise and trial", but believed she had discharged a religious duty.[3]

More informally, the Quaker community was, as time went on, increasingly strengthened by widespread ties through marriage. For instance, Francis Fox married a Friend from Settle in Yorkshire and in his will he left small bequests to family connections in Bristol, Salisbury and Cornwall as well as Plymouth. The interconnections between the families of Collier, Cookworthy, Croker, Fox, Hingston and Prideaux provide a happy hunting ground for genealogists.

Locally, in 1697 Plymouth was in discussion with Kingsbridge about establishing a First Day meeting for worship at Holbeton. We gather that such a meeting started because eighteen months later it was agreed that the housing for Friends' horses there was to be given up.[4] Later there was a small meeting at Modbury.

If a Meeting was in difficulties it would be helped out. In 1690 money was raised for Exeter Meeting House, and in 1791 for the completion of Cullompton Meeting House.[5] It was not only local Meetings that would be helped. In 1743, when the Meeting House at Wellingborough burnt down, a collection was taken up to help with the rebuilding, and when it was thought that the collection had not raised enough, it was renewed. Nor was it only other Meetings. In 1736 assistance was given to Thomas Bowden of Exeter, said to be the victim of a malicious prosecution.[6]

The minute books from this period give us a partial view of the life of Plymouth Meeting. Basically the Men's minutes tell us mainly about permission for marriages, disputes, disciplinary action, collections for various purposes, and sending representatives to the Quarterly Meeting. The Women's minutes tell us mainly about regular disbursements and marriages. While the disputes and the steps taken to deal with erring Friends may be interesting, they do not give a rounded account of what was going on. And not everything was recorded. The minutes do not at this time mention deaths or tell us that the agreed marriages actually happened. Sufferings, which from now on mainly meant distraints for tithes, (though this changed towards the end of the century, as explained below) were recorded separately, to be sent up to London. Select Quarterly and Monthly Meeting for Elders and Overseers were established during this period and these included men and women together.[7] The ordinary Monthly Meetings met regularly, but often had little business to conduct. And perhaps the men themselves found the business less than compelling. In February 1694, there being only three Friends present, they deplored Friends' "remissness in coming to Monthly Meetings for the maintaining and upholding the service of truth" and went on to desire "that all Friends who have received a sense of truth might in the fear of God be stirred up to more diligence in this weighty concern."

In 1770, Friends living at "the Dock" (Devonport) put a proposal to the Monthly Meeting about holding a meeting locally. The Monthly Meeting thought that, as it was just a private evening meeting in their own houses, it did not need their approval, but there might be advantages in holding it.[8]

From time to time there were property issues to consider: complaints about the high rent of the burial ground on the Hoe and an eventual decision to give it up in 1721;[9] unruly tenants given notice to quit, then allowed to continue on promise of good behaviour, then given notice again;[10] acquisition of the freehold of the property, first offered in 1693, but not carried through until 1703 when Henry Ceane acquired it personally and offered it to the Meeting, completing the transaction in December 1704;[11] and repairs and improvements to the building, first repairs for which a collection was raised in 1696, then a new roof in 1722 for which there was another collection, and then in 1736 the provision of a porch for the front door of the Meeting House, which was too exposed to the weather, this porch to be done "in a handsome manner".[12] The picture from this is of a prosperous meeting being run by men of business, and this picture continues for most of the rest of its history, though there is little information on the part played by the majority of the members. The other feature which was to be evident throughout later history was a certain restlessness in the Meeting's relationships with its property.

Clearly they were assiduous in taking care of the poor amongst them. This was particularly a duty of the Women's Monthly Meeting, and from time to time they had to tell the Men's Monthly Meeting that they did not have enough money for the purpose, whereupon the Men would give them a small allocation out of what was called the "public stock". The Women's Meeting typically gave money month after month to maintain the same few poor Quakers. In addition they paid one of them for cleaning, presumably the Meeting House. The Men's Meeting also gave grants to impoverished individuals, but these were not regular payments. For instance, in 1694, two Friends were appointed to visit Grace Merchant and give her some supply if it were needed. But those who had got into difficulty through rashness or negligence were another matter, though traders who defaulted on their debts were not at first condemned as they later were. When, in 1722, James Chapple fell into difficulties, probably because of illness, Friends were willing to do something for him, provided that he sold his household goods to pay his debts. The need for help was removed by his death.[13] This contrasts with the treatment of Matthew Thwaite 45 years later. Friends inspected his affairs and made a distribution to his creditors, but still declared themselves out of unity with him.[14]

Because of the obligation of mutual support, the Quakers wanted to know for whom they might be responsible, and this evolved, among the Society at large, into a formal membership system. The Yearly Meeting first produced a definition of membership in 1737. In addition to their responsibility for each other, they wanted to disown those people who might otherwise bring them into disrepute. Occasional cases of this came before the Men's Monthly Meeting. For instance, in 1717 a couple were accused of fornication and adultery. They admitted it and did not repent, so a public testimony against them was read out and published, in order that the rest of Plymouth would know that such behaviour was not condoned.

Some idea of how things worked, or did not work, may be gathered from incidents in the lives of William and Jacob Cookworthy. William Cookworthy is mainly known in Plymouth as the first person in Britain to work out how to make porcelain, as the discoverer of China Clay in Cornwall, and as the initiator of a short-lived porcelain factory, but he was a very active Quaker. He was born into a Quaker family in Kingsbridge in 1705. His father, also William Cookworthy, a weaver, who was active among Kingsbridge Friends, died shortly after being present at Plymouth Monthly Meeting in third month 1719. At the age of 15 the younger William was apprenticed to Sylvanus Bevan, a London apothecary who was also a Quaker.[15] No-one seems to know how this came about, but it was not unusual for a Quaker tradesman to take an apprentice from a distressed Quaker family – this was one of the mechanisms by which the Quakers cared for their own. What was unusual was the distance. Cookworthy walked to London. He took to the apothecary work so well that the Bevan brothers accepted him into partnership, and within a short time he came to Plymouth to set up a branch of the firm of Bevans and Cookworthy, in Notte Street.

Cookworthy first appeared at the Plymouth Men's Monthly Meeting in tenth month 1735, nine years after his arrival in Plymouth, when he was seeking permission to marry Sarah Berry, the daughter of a

Taunton Friend. As was usual, Friends were appointed to enquire whether either party had any other commitments, and the marriage was then allowed.[16] From then on he was a frequent attender at the Monthly Meeting, though it was not for another ten years that he was recognised as a minister. In 1745, when the Monthly Meeting was worried (not for the first time) about "disorderly proceeding" at the Meeting for Worship, he was one of three Friends appointed to draw up a paper on the subject, and when the paper was approved he was asked to read it at the end of the afternoon Meeting.[17] His wife Sarah first attended the Women's Monthly Meeting in 1737 and came regularly thereafter.

Meanwhile his younger brother Jacob had also appeared on the scene. In September 1742 he complained to the Monthly Meeting that Joseph Veal of Austell had been courting Elizabeth Hingston, with whom he had an engagement of marriage. The Meeting found that the parties "not fully explaining themselves at the first about the settlement, a disagreement ensued, upon which the intended match broke off." A Friend called Thomas Jewell recorded his dissent, holding that there was an engagement. Jacob appealed to the Quarterly meeting, which first came down on his side, as Elizabeth's father, James Hingston, a member of a prominent Quaker family at Holbeton, had behaved improperly, but at a later meeting "tenderly and unanimously" recommended Jacob to make an end of the difference.[18] What we cannot know, unless further evidence comes to light, is whether those concerned gave full vent to their indignation, or whether it was hidden under the guise of sobriety and waiting upon the inward light – most likely some compromise between the two.

The problem for young Quaker men and women, including Jacob, was that of finding acceptable Quakers to marry, within a fairly limited circle, as "marrying out" was likely to be contrary to the advice of parents and Friends, which could lead to disownment, particularly if the other party wanted a church or chapel wedding. He did, however, find a bride in Sarah Morris of Kingsbridge a few years later.

On the death of his wife in September 1745, William Cookworthy had a spiritual crisis which led to him retreating from the world for several months, at Looe, and thereafter withdrawing from the day to day running of his business. It was following this that he came forward as a Quaker minister and from time to time travelled in the ministry in the West Country.[19]

The question which William Cookworthy first took up after his spiritual upheaval was that of dealing in prize goods. For over 40 years of the 18th century Britain was engaged in a series of wars, and because of Plymouth's development as a naval base this had two effects on its trade. One was that the town's normal sea-borne trade declined, as ship-owners avoided Plymouth for fear of their sailors being lured[20] or pressed into the Navy. The other resulted from naval vessels and privateers bringing into port the prizes they had captured, ships of the enemy nations, together with the goods they carried. These would be auctioned, and local merchants could do very well out of buying up the goods and selling them on.[21] It is perhaps understandable that a Quaker merchant, finding other opportunities restricted, might attend these auctions at Plymouth or elsewhere. Although actually having shares in privateers was unequivocally condemned by the London Yearly Meeting of Friends, the ultimate decision-making body, nothing was decided about prize goods.

By 1746 some attempt had been made to raise the question with the central Quaker bodies, because in that year Devon Quarterly Meeting minuted that "as the Meeting for Sufferings have given no satisfactory answer to the question about dealing in prize goods, the Friends of Plymouth do desire it may be proposed to the Yearly Meeting."[22] This is actually the first mention of the issue in either the Monthly or the Quarterly Meeting. In July 1747 Plymouth Monthly

Meeting came back to the topic, saying that as the question had been put too generally, it should be put more specifically: "Can it be judged consistent with our known principles against wars and fighting, for Friends to attend sales of Prize Goods or deal for them with the captors or their agents?" However, the next Quarterly Meeting, at which Cookworthy was present, decided that "as the matter lies already before the Yearly Meeting it is most advisable to rest it there." It should be noted, however, that there is no evidence in the minutes of the Meeting for Sufferings or of the Yearly Meeting that either body ever considered the issue. This may perhaps be explained by the fact that in 1748 Devonshire's London Correspondent on the Meeting for Sufferings, Thomas Reynolds, was removed for non-attendance. Communications had simply not been getting through. [23]

Plymouth Friends then decided to accept the judgment of the Quarterly Meeting, upon which Cookworthy wrote a lengthy note of dissent in the minute book, starting with a statement about his own religious experience: "As I am thoroughly convinced (having had a measure of experience) of the excellence and saving power of that Divine Principle of Light and Life which we as a people have to profess and hold forth . . . . so am I equally satisfied that the various branches of our testimony are real shoots from the Root of Life. . . . And that [testimony] against war and fighting appearing to my understanding as one of the most considerable importance, I have found myself engaged to contribute as much as in me lay towards its support, and it seeming also very clear to me that those Friends who attend sales of prize goods do give up this testimony by a public acknowledgment of the rightfulness of the acquisitions which are made contrary to it, I have found myself engaged to oppose this practice. . . ."[24] He had made his point. In 1758 the Queries were revised to include a specific mention of dealing in prize goods – whether this was due to Cookworthy's pursuit of the issue is uncertain, but it probably contributed. And in 1807, when Plymouth and Kingsbridge Monthly Meeting was asked to visit a Friend, Thomas Coates, who was a member of Gracechurch Street Meeting in London, he was confronted on two issues. One was his failure to attend meeting, which he partly remedied, the other was his trading in prize goods. He admitted that he knew he was doing wrong, but said that he could only put a stop to it by getting out of the partnership of which he was a member.[25]

William Cookworthy tended to play a significant part in dealing with those who erred from the Quaker way, by not attending meeting, "walking disorderly", or marrying contrary to the advice or customs of Friends. The testimony concerning him, which Plymouth Friends wrote at his death, mentioned that he was concerned to reclaim offenders not by severity but by convincing them of the impropriety of the consequences of their actions. "In all cases the tenderness and love which so eminently marked the performance of his religious and social duty were never suspended."[26] These disciplinary cases occurred from time to time, and there are three for which there is a bit of evidence besides what appears in the minutes. In 1758 Cookworthy and John Fox were asked to deal with Jonathan Hancock, who had been married by a priest to a woman "not of the Society". Early in 1759 they brought him to a Monthly Meeting where he was "tenderly dealt with", but was in no way aware of his conduct being faulty. A month later, however, Cookworthy brought a paper written by him. This paper asked for charitable dealing, and said, "I broke through those wholesome Disciplines which are ordained for the support of the Society by marrying out to the Church of England without consent of Parents or approbation of Friends." He later mentioned his "carnal inclinations" and referred to his action as a Crime. He ended with "the fervent desire of my heart to follow the same worship & faith that you profess, knowing it aright in the sight of God." The paper was ordered to be read at the end of the afternoon Meeting. This was the usual method of bringing such matters to a conclusion. If there had been no recantation or an insufficient one, a statement composed by the Monthly Meeting would be read, also at the end of the afternoon meeting, dissociating Friends from the offender. His abject statement ended the matter for the time being, but from 1768 he was in trouble again for failing to attend the public meeting for worship, for disorderly behaviour and frequenting ale houses and taverns, and above all for not meeting his written financial commitments to the children of his first wife. After a protracted process, during which he treated the Monthly Meeting with "insolence", he was in 1771 declared not to be in unity with Friends.[27]

Where women were concerned, the Women's Meeting, if they were warned in advance, tried to prevent marrying out, usually to no avail.

In 1775 Thomas Binns and J Sparkes of Exeter wrote to Charles Fox in Plymouth, addressing him as "Dear Cousin", reporting that the daughter of Geo. Price has been married by a Priest, and asking for Plymouth Friends to take the necessary steps "according to the Rules of the Society" and inform them of the result. In this case Plymouth could only reply that Ann Price had now moved to Newton within the compass of Exeter Monthly Meeting.[28]

The third case is that of Mary Wakeham. At the Monthly Meeting of 6th month 1780, a letter was received from Mary Wakam (her spelling) acknowledging her misconduct in walking contrary to the rules of our Society, and expressing her hope and trust that "the almighty goodness will be mercifully pleased to pass by my offence and enable me the remaining part of my life to walk more circumspectly." This is the first mention of her in either the Women's or the Men's Monthly Meeting, and neither the letter nor the minute tells us what she has done wrong. The letter was left before the meeting, and the matter continued from one month to the next for almost a year until in 5th month 1781 (when her name was now spelled Wakeham) it was ordered that the letter be read at the end of the afternoon meeting. Ten years later she was attending the Women's Monthly Meeting, so her rehabilitation was complete. During the time that her letter lay before the Monthly Meeting, William Cookworthy died.[29]

Despite all the concern about marrying within the Society,

Cookworthy's life demonstrates that Plymouth Quakers were by no means isolated from the world or tied up in their businesses. After the period of retirement which marked his crisis, he reduced the amount of time he spent on his business, leaving it in the hands of others, and devoted himself more to scientific enquiries, carrying on an extensive correspondence, which gave him a national reputation as an inventor and geological chemist. His conversation on a variety of topics informed and delighted a wide variety of people, both residents of the town and those passing through. On the less worldly side, he also had an interest in the Swedish mystic Emanuel Swedenborg and translated some of his works. Since then, there has been an intermittent interest in Swedenborg among some Friends on both sides of the Atlantic, and in the later 19th century a Quaker, Charles William Dymond, was lecturing on him in Plymouth. None of his activities in any way detracted from Cookworthy's standing among Friends. He died in 1780, having already sold his porcelain business and the patent. In the 1950s, when Quaker remains, including those of Cookworthy, were removed from the old Charles Street burial ground and re-interred at Efford, there was a successful campaign to stop his remains being put into a common grave with the others, though Plymouth Quakers did insist on his grave being as modest as the others in their part of the cemetery.[30]

John Collier's diary for 1790-91, ten years after William Cookworthy's death, also demonstrates that Friends were mingling with the rest of Plymouth society. At this stage he was going to Meeting twice on Sundays, finding business meetings tedious, upholding the testimony against smuggling while setting up his new business dealing in wine, and getting appointed as a member of what he called the Slave Committee, which was probably the committee of the Plymouth Society for Effecting the Abolition of the Slave Trade, of which other Quakers would also have been members; but he was also joining mixed parties of Anglicans and Quakers in social outings, reading widely in fiction, poetry and political works, dressing in fine clothes, going to the theatre (possibly surreptitiously), and joining other younger Quakers to teach in the Sunday school which the Rev. Robert Hawker had established at Charles Church. This was not what we think of as a Sunday school, but a school for poor children to give them a basic education – admittedly so that they could read the scriptures.[31]

Presumably some of these activities helped to bring down on him a lambasting from a travelling minister, Sally Tuckett, from Looe. He recorded, "Sally Tuckett, Elizabeth Fox, & Amy Berry drank tea with us, purposely I suppose to have a Meeting with the family; accordingly as soon as tea things were removed they fished for silence & I as often hacked in a conversation, but at last . . . we settled with a silence until it was interrupted by a discourse from S. Tuckett – Jobation on Jobation followed, we were addressed all round particularly Father & Myself, she hoped there would be a time when like the Prodigal Son I should know a returning to my Father's House & be clothed in purple."[32]

In 1802 John Collier was one of the subscribers to the rebuilding of the Meeting House, contributing the very respectable sum of £25, but two years later he was visited for not attending meeting. After a couple of visits he wrote a letter expressing his desire to be no longer considered a member of the Society of Friends. The Monthly Meeting left this letter to the next meeting, but then concluded that they would not continue him as a member any longer. When John Collier was elected to parliament 28 years later, he did, however, continue to pursue Quaker causes.[33]

As for numbers in Plymouth Meeting for the 18th century we have only the births and burials to go by. In the three years 1680 – 82 there were eight births recorded and four burials; in 1730 – 32 there were six births recorded and nine burials; and in 1780 – 82 there were six births recorded, of whom two were in Tavistock and one in Bere Ferrers, and three burials. 1820 is the first year for which I have found actual numbers of members. There were 146 members of Plymouth meeting, of whom 91 were female. It is apparent that children were included in these figures.[34]

It is difficult to be certain about the children and their education. Among the Queries which the Monthly Meetings were required to answer to the Quarterly Meeting, was a general question: Is care taken about the education of the children? This could simply be answered with a Yes, which tells us little. It seems likely that schooling either made use of local resources or was done privately. If this were the case, it would imply another means of integration into the life of the town. Devon Friends did, however, give financial support to Ackworth School when it was set up in 1779 under the aegis of the Yearly Meeting, but this was for the children of those who could not afford education otherwise, and was a long distance away in West Yorkshire. They likewise supported Sidcot School in Somerset when it was re-started for the poorer West Country Quaker children in 1808, and this was certainly used to some extent.[35]

Towards the end of the 18th century, Friends had started to take an interest in the education of the poorer people of Plymouth. In 1787 Robert Hawker, the vicar of Charles Church, had started a Sunday school, in which, as we have seen, some Quakers were involved. A "school of industry" grew out of the Sunday school four years later, merging with a girls' school, which may have been the school of industry in which "Quaker ladies", including a Mary Fox, were heavily involved, and collected money for. The school of industry provided a basic education for the manual trades. By 1798 it had its own building, the "Household of Faith", which overlooked the Quaker burial ground. [36]

In 1785, Kingsbridge Monthly Meeting, after a long series of meetings in which nothing much was recorded, suggested a union with Plymouth, on the grounds that it would be of service to both meetings, "particularly with respect to Discipline". This was put to Plymouth Monthly Meeting, which, after asking for time to consider, quickly agreed, and the proposal was put to the Quarterly Meeting. The Women's Meetings were not consulted about it, merely informed afterwards. The Quarterly Meeting agreed, and at the same meeting went on to approve a similar union of Exeter, Cullompton and Spiceland; this seems to have left a single struggling meeting on its own in the north of the county. From now on, Monthly Meetings were held alternately at Plymouth and Kingsbridge, and each of the particular meetings agreed to hold a Preparatory Meeting in advance. These were very soon re-labelled as Preparative Meetings, and the Plymouth and Kingsbridge Monthly Meeting came to be re-labelled as the Western Division of Devonshire. The main function of the Preparative Meetings at this time was to prepare the answers to the Queries that Monthly Meetings had to answer.[37] The Monthly Meetings were to be held on Fourth Days (Wednesdays) at 9 a.m., which meant that they could not be attended by those who did not have control over their own affairs. Nevertheless from now on the minutes occasionally note the presence of Friends "not under appointment", and this was also the case with the Preparative Meetings.

Towards the end of the century, the war with France began to make an impact on Friends. In addition to the usual distraints on Friends in country parishes, who had animals or crops taken away for non-payment of tithes or church rates (so-called, as the record always added), some of them also had fines for refusing to convey the baggage of soldiers, and there were also Friends in Plymouth who had property distrained for non-payment of what was called the Rate for manning of (the) Navy. This rate, starting around 1795 was only levied in certain parishes where the government offered men a bounty for joining the Navy. The Overseers of the Poor, who paid the bounty, were entitled to add to the poor rate in order to cover the payment, and it was this additional charge which the Yearly Meeting urged Friends not to pay. The government did recognise the Quaker position in one respect: any Overseer of the Poor who was also a Quaker would not be fined for refusing to offer the bounty, and Justices of the Peace were to appoint a deputy to do it. This Navy rate did not become regular. There might also be distraints for refusing to pay for substitutes in the militia, or for refusing to pay the rates which supported the bounty paid to those volunteering for the militia. Distraint, of course, caused disruption, and there was an additional charge to cover the cost of collection. Friends consistently claimed that the constable or other officer took goods to a value greater than what was owed, though sometimes a conscientious constable returned the difference.[38] In December 1793 the Quarterly Meeting was warning Monthly Meetings to make sure that the Overseers of the Poor were dividing the rate for paying the bounties from the ordinary poor rate, as this was not being done in some parishes.

On the question of "sufferings", something that did not happen: on 12th March 1789, there was a day of public rejoicing for George III's recovery from illness. In Exeter six Friends had their windows broken by the mob because those windows were not illuminated. Nothing of the sort was recorded in Plymouth.[39]

In addition, in February 1801 the Monthly Meeting received a letter from Bristol Friends concerning one of their members, Joseph Mevety, who was believed to be on one of the ships of war at Plymouth. Friends were appointed to meet with him, but, for whatever reason, it was not until October that they were able to report that they had done so. They said that he showed "so much tenderness and sensibility, with apparent dissatisfaction at his present situation on board the Cambridge Ship of War" that they judged it was a case meriting further care. The matter came to an end, as far as Plymouth was concerned, in January of the following year when the entire ship's company of the Cambridge (which was the flagship of the Port Admiral) was paid off, Joseph Mevety among them.[40]

At this point it is useful to say something about the development of Quaker beliefs, particularly as it helps to introduce the next chapter. It might be argued that the early Quakers did not have beliefs, they had experiences. We have seen that this approach was still alive in the

1740s when William Cookworthy appealed to his experience to justify an unpopular stance. Their experiences, however, often conflicted with orthodox beliefs, and the Quaker preachers were eager to point to the differences. The central experience was of an inward contact with something that was variously called the Seed, the inward Light, the Spirit of God, the Guide, or other names. They maintained that this contact, and the guidance which came from it was available to everyone, though the gifts which it gave might differ. Following the guidance, the leadings of the spirit, could lead to a life without sin.

From this starting point came many consequences. There was a belief in equality before God, an equality which in theory included women. In life lived by the spirit, there would be a single standard of truth, so Quakers would not take oaths, which implied a double standard (besides contravening Jesus's commandment not to swear). They held that it was not necessary to have been educated at Oxford or Cambridge to be a minister, and they refused to pay tithes to men they called hireling priests. The church was not a building but the community of convinced men and women. The building they called a steeplehouse. Communion and baptism were understood in a spiritual sense and not as ritual acts. Pacifism was not among the earliest stands taken, but in 1662 a public statement was issued by the Quaker leadership, and thereafter it was adhered to.

There was gradual evolution in what Quakers proclaimed. The assertion of perfectibility was quietly dropped, though the belief in God in everyone was not. The insistence on simplicity and plainness of dress could be taken to extremes, and one leading Quaker, Margaret Fell, protested against it. As time went on, it became increasingly difficult to generalise about Quaker beliefs, because of the diffusion of Quakerism over other continents. By the middle of the 18th century, Plymouth Quakers, along with others, were fully into what has been labelled as the Quietist period. This may be exemplified by the Colchester Friend, John Kendall who wrote in 1763: "As we are not able, by our weak capacities, to judge of things rightly, the best way for us is to leave the event to the disposal of the all-wise Providence."[40.] However, this increased emphasis on acceptance of God's will did not stop scientific enquiry or commercial enterprise and innovation. In 1788 the same John Kendall wrote an extended letter to Friends of the Counties of Devon and Cornwall; and Plymouth and Kingsbridge Monthly Meeting thought sufficiently well of this letter to copy it into their minute book and ask for it to be read in meetings. Among the advice given, he twice mentioned the dangers which attended upon too great an application to the acquisition of worldly comforts. Perhaps in his travels he had noticed this as a problem among the prosperous Friends of the south-west.

From the late 18th century, Quakers would be considerably influenced by the evangelical movements in Britain. Their views became more orthodox, with greater emphasis on original sin, to the extent that some Friends even came to deny the central Quaker belief in the light of God in everyone, though it is not clear whether this was the case in Plymouth. One of the features of this trend was that evangelical Quakers came to feel a strong bond with evangelicals in other denominations, and, as will be seen, this was a development in Plymouth.[42]. However, when some Yearly Meetings in America called a conference to put together a declaration which came near to being a creed, the British drew back. They had sent delegates to the conference, but they would not adhere to a declaration. At the end of the 19th century, another conference in this country, held at Manchester, epitomised and reinforced the move towards "liberal" Quakerism which has persisted ever since. The evangelical movement was one of the driving forces of the philanthropy which became prominent in the 19th century.

Chapter 4

Philanthropy and evangelism: 1800 to 1890

Plymouth expanded rapidly in the first half of the 19th century, its population more than tripling from 16,040 in 1801 to 52,221 in 1851. It overtook Devonport, which had had 7,000 more inhabitants in 1801, but had 14,000 fewer in 1851, and, moreover, was losing members of the "opulent classes". Stonehouse, which had always been the smallest of the three towns, tripled in size, ending up with almost 12,000 in 1851. The number of houses in Plymouth went from 1,744 to 5,178. Of course, the population was not evenly distributed among the houses. In 1847 it was said that in some parts there were 70, 80 or even 90 people living in the same house, and 11,000 people living in single rooms. At this time some 60% of the population was under 24. As for the sanitary arrangements, there were 27 streets with no drainage, and another 53 with inadequate drainage, while 753 houses did not get the town water supply. In Market Alley there were 158 people using the same privy.[1] There were cholera epidemics in 1832 and 1849, after which some action was taken on sanitation. We have to envisage large numbers of uneducated people, mostly children or young adults, living in squalor.

Quakers did respond to this situation, mostly, but not exclusively, in the educational field. But their response was as individuals and was not mentioned in the minutes of the business meetings of the Society. In those meetings the first major business of the century was on another property issue, and, once again, any discussions that led up to it were not recorded.

In March 1802, the male Quakers of Plymouth called a special meeting to consider "the propriety of erecting a new meeting house for the use of Friends in Plymouth." The next sentence of the minute seems tentative: "It appears to be the sense of this meeting that such a building shall at a proper time be erected on the site of the present one." Pledges of money were given at the meeting, and a committee set up to seek more subscriptions. The largest subscription came from Francis Fox who pledged £150 and later increased it to £200. He was followed by two Friends from London, Wilson Birkbeck and Hannah Plumstead (his wife), who gave £100 each. Apart from a subscription from a Friend in Bristol, all the other contributions came from Friends in the local Meeting, and there was no call on other Meetings in Devon. The new Treville Street building was brought into use in August 1804, and the final recorded cost was £1249 1s 3d, including a wall to the street, paving, new end walls to adjoining houses, and the rent of a house meantime. This, however, was a net cost, as "the old Dwelling House" was sold to one of the builders for a £15 reduction in his account, and the old benches, valued at two guineas, went to a carpenter who then made no charge for the back porch doors.[2] Even with the disposal of the dwelling house, the Meeting House itself did not take up the whole of the site, as part of it was later sold off to the Preparative Meeting and used for the Adult School. In 1806 it was thought proper to put something in the Preparative Meeting minutes about all this, and an amended version of the original minute was copied in, with some later details added.

When the Quarterly Meeting ordered a collection to be taken up from the constituent meetings, it was always for a fixed amount of twenty pounds, though several collections might be ordered at once. This twenty pounds would be divided among the individual meetings. In 1808 the Plymouth Preparative Meeting noted that as Kingsbridge meeting had declined in numbers, its members were having to pay more than their fair share of a collection, and it agreed to increase its own share of the twenty pounds to nine pounds six shillings, leaving Kingsbridge four pounds and six shillings to pay.[3] So at this time Plymouth was paying nearly half the total amount of a collection, while Plymouth and Kingsbridge between them were paying 70% of it.

The Francis Fox mentioned as contributing to the rebuilding was a grandson of William Cookworthy, and, with three partners, was carrying on Cookworthy's old business as a druggist. In his younger days he wore clothing "something nearer the fashion of the world", but found this led him into too many temptations and difficulties, so amended it. He was appointed as an elder at a comparatively early age, and was recognised as a minister. His place in Plymouth history is secured by his philanthropic efforts for the poor of Plymouth and in particular his collaboration with others, both non-Quaker and Quaker, but especially Henry Woollcombe, a prominent solicitor who had a hand in various improvement projects, in setting up the Plymouth Public Free School in 1809. Its first title was "Institution for the education and improvement of the morals of poor children." In the prospectus for subscribers, the largest letters were reserved for the improvement of morals.[4]

The school was set up on the monitorial system of another Quaker, Joseph Lancaster, with older pupils (monitors) instructing the younger. Lancaster was in correspondence with Woollcombe giving advice. [5] The main aim of the evangelical Quakers, those in Plymouth probably among them, was not so much to improve the children's chances in this world as to secure their salvation in the next, by improving their morals (as stated in the title of the school) and enabling them to read the Bible. Fox died unexpectedly in 1812, and the Committee reported in 1813 that "Your Committee cannot but advert to the loss which the Institution has sustained by the death of several excellent persons among the Subscribers for the last year. Among them, it is with particular regret that your Committee have to include the name of Francis Fox, to whose benevolent exertions the Institution is so highly indebted. . . . Your Committee, anxious to testify the respect and attachment they felt to his memory, attended the burial as your representatives. . . ." The list of subscribers to the school included several recognisably Quaker names, and in 1812 the Secretary was a Quaker, Benjamin Balkwill (a partner of Fox in the druggist business), who was dating the minutes in Quaker style, but adding the name of the month in brackets. He continued in this post to 1845.[6]

In the jokey rules of Henry Woollcombe's small "club", among the restrictions imposed on members, it was laid down that Francis Fox was "not to allow his benevolence to outweigh his reason". With other members of this club, Fox was also concerned with another initiative, to provide housing for the poor, in Shute Park, just to the north of the town walls. Although money was raised, this venture came to nothing, possibly because of Fox's sudden death.[7]

When Francis Fox died, it was reported in a local paper that "his funeral took place on the 25th inst [September], and was attended by about 250 persons; he was carried underhanded by eight Quakers to the Burial-Ground in Broad St. The procession closed with the committees of the public schools and public institutions to which he was a liberal benefactor. Out of respect to the memory of their townsman, all the shops through which the funeral passed, from the house in Frank Row to the grave, were closely shut as a testimony how highly his virtues both public and private were appreciated." An anonymous informant added that "the magistrates of Plymouth requested they might walk in the procession in form with their robes, as on public occasions; this Friends did not think proper to consent to but they attended the funeral."[8]

The Monthly Meeting recorded a testimony concerning Francis Fox. Their reason for doing so, they said, was that "religious advantage is often derived to posterity in holding up to view the character of the righteous". After describing his services to other Quakers, they recorded that "in him the Christian character shone with peculiar brightness, evincing that true religion, which operates by purifying the heart, necessarily produces works of righteousness – The prominent features of his mind were, love to God, and goodwill to Man. . . . Deeply interested in things connected with the welfare of his fellow creatures, he was a liberal & zealous promoter of public works of benevolence: to the poor and wretched of every description he was an unwearied but unostentatious benefactor, and justly attributing many of the evils which exist in this class of society, to the want of right instruction in early life, he was earnestly and successfully engaged in extending this blessing to the poor children of his native town."[9]

Up to the end, Francis Fox did not expect his illness to be fatal, but all Quakers were (and are) urged to make and review their wills in time of health, and he had accordingly both made and revised his will in previous years. After dealing with his ordinary bequests, he made a special use of the sum of £3000 which he expected his heirs to receive on the death of his widowed sister-in-law, Elizabeth Cookworthy. (His brother had changed his name to Cookworthy, out of respect to his maternal grandfather, who had had no sons.) This sum he left on trust divided into three parts. The largest sum was for the construction and maintenance of six houses to provide accommodation for 12 poor women over the age of 50, the next was to go to the support of the Plymouth Free School, and the last to establish a relief fund for poor members of the Society of Friends in Devon and Cornwall. The sum for providing housing proved insufficient, and was made up by his daughter Sarah who had married William Dillworth Crewdson of Kendal. This charity remains in existence under the name of Fox and Crewdson's.

Various bits of information in the minutes help us to form some sort of picture of the Meeting in the first quarter of the 19th century. Two meetings for worship were held on Sundays, and at least one during the week. There were newcomers from time to time, because Friends were appointed to show them where to sit. A second Sarah Abbott, second wife of John Abbott, was frequently touring other parts of the country as a travelling minister. Disownment of Friends, declaring them not to be in unity, occurred from time to time, mainly for non-attendance, but when they went off to other denominations, the wording could be gentler than it used to be. Of Margaret Fox junior it was said that "we feel much love towards her and sincerely desire her advancement in that religious course which we do not consider to be essentially connected with external forms but is of an inward, spiritual and unchangeable nature." [10]

In 1828, the Monthly Meeting reported, in response to enquiry from London, that it had nine children of non-members who were "in low circumstances", of whom two boys were at Sidcot School. Plymouth Meeting at this time was contributing about £11 a year to Sidcot School, later reducing to about £8 a year.

At about this time there is evidence that Quakers in Falmouth and Plymouth were engaged in helping refugees fleeing from the Portuguese Civil War of 1828, "receiving them with warm fraternity". They provided the refugees with shoes and clothing, and a school for the younger ones to enable them "to read and write and know the Christian doctrine". [11]

The picture of a smoothly running, well-organised, if declining Quaker meeting, is disrupted only by the continued restlessness over property matters. Early in the century, there were difficulties over the burial ground, with the Monthly Meeting advising Plymouth Friends to make a correct plan of it, and later Joseph Cookworthy, who was a property trustee though no longer a member, refusing to sign a deed for new trustees because he disapproved of the way in which graves had been dealt with. Later still, but by 1839, male Friends, without going through any business meeting, acquired three properties in Norley Lane adjacent to the Meeting House – but then the Preparative Meeting had to deal with problems, including boundary disputes with neighbours, one of whom was a Quaker who seems to have got her way by being appropriately non-confrontational. The property producing no income, it was eventually sold. [12]

By 1823, the number of Friends in Tavistock had increased to the point where the Quarterly Meeting could agree to establish a Meeting there. It was agreed it should have its own Preparative Meeting, but by

1854 this had been given up, and there was a Plymouth and Tavistock Preparative Meeting, though Tavistock was hardly ever represented. Tavistock Meeting continued till the end of 1873, and the Monthly Meetings were held there about once a year.

The question of dealing in prize goods was the last one which Plymouth Friends took up nationally; but they were assiduous in responding to the national campaigns, from that against slavery to that against the Contagious Diseases Act (which in effect persecuted prostitutes but not their clients).

In the second half of the 19th century, Plymouth Meeting began to change. The change is best introduced by looking at one of the Friends who made a considerable contribution to the business life of the town, Edward James. He had moved to Plymouth from Redruth in about 1832 and set up in partnership with William Bryant, who had been convinced and accepted into membership in 1832, starting a business in the town, at first as general merchants, also in 1832. As Bryant and James, they went on to start a soap factory, and later patented improvements in blacking (probably boot blacking). Their agent in London for "patent India rubber oil and blacking" was Francis May, another Quaker, and in 1844 Bryant and May teamed up together in London as a grocery firm which went on to import safety matches and then manufacture them. Bryant's family originally stayed in Plymouth, where his daughter Edith Ellen died in 1852, but by 1861 they had moved to Kingston upon Thames. Edward James, who had set up his own starch factory as an independent business, stayed in Plymouth and eventually employed a large workforce.[14] He was, moreover, involved at an early stage in the new Quaker Adult School.

The Adult School started in 1861. Compared with some Meetings in other parts of the country, Plymouth Friends were late in starting on such a venture. The Friends First Day School Association had been set up in 1847, and though it was mainly for junior schools at the beginning, it was soon dominated by the adult schools. Nor was it the first such initiative in Plymouth. In December 1813 a public meeting had been held to set up an association, and an Adult School may have been started which lasted till about 1822.[15] The Schools were originally for Bible reading, with writing and arithmetic being added, then the curriculum gradually broadening out.

There is no information on where the Plymouth Quaker impulse came from. Fifty years later, the School Council recorded that the Adult School started on 25th August 1861. Edward James died at the end of 1870, and when Friends came to write about him they said that "in no situation did his character as a Christian shine more brightly than in that of Superintendent of the Friends Adult First Day School. The interest that he felt in this work was very great; he seemed deeply concerned for the spiritual and temporal welfare of the Scholars, and after the usual reading of a chapter at the close of the School, would often address them in an earnest and solemn manner, inviting them to come to Jesus, and to show by their daily lives on whose side they were." James may have been the first Superintendent of the school, and he or his family may have been among the moving forces behind it. For some years afterwards his daughter Charlotte M James was the secretary of the school, and when she died it was said that the school was "one of the great objects of her life."[16]

In 1856 trustees for the Meeting House had sold to Charles Prideaux, who was acting on behalf of the Preparative Meeting, some property adjoining the Meeting House, though this was not recorded in any minutes. The property consisted of at least two linked buildings on at least three floors, on the corner of Treville Street and Charles Street. Old photographs show it in this position, on a level slightly below the Meeting House. In 1871, some work was done on this property to adapt it for the First Day Schools, at a cost of over £2000. They occupied parts of the two upper floors. In addition to the schoolroom there were at least three classrooms. The work included a "portable partition" and a platform, which seems to indicate that the schoolroom was used in a formal manner. There was a door into the Meeting House. Other parts of the combined building were let out commercially. The mortgage on the property was paid off in 1887, and in 1888, with more room being needed for the Adult School, notice was given to a tenant to move out of the upper floors of one house, though she was to retain the ground floor.[17]

In 1874 the Monthly Meeting, which by now consisted only of Plymouth Meeting, decided that it ought to pay attention to the adult school work which was being done in Friends' name. It agreed on various measures: Friends not engaged in teaching should visit the school occasionally; there should be an annual meeting of Friends to consider the affairs of the school, in addition to the quarterly meetings of teachers; there should be a meeting once a month for simple religious instruction; and two new groups should be formed. These were an association for distributing, lending and exchanging tracts, and a Friends Temperance Society.[18]

In the following year, the Monthly Meeting received a report. The First Day Adult School was held from 8.30 to 10 in the morning, with an average attendance of 65 men and 30 women. There were nine teachers. Peripheral activities had sprouted. There was a mothers' meeting on Second Day (Monday), 3 to 5 p.m., with an attendance of about 30. A Mission Meeting was held at Westbrook, the home of R (Richard) Reynolds Fox and his wife Frances Elizabeth, out in the country, as it then was, on the way to Tamerton Foliot. This was on First Day evenings, with 30 to 40 attending. In the winter, a night school was held for girls from 8 to 9.30, with attendance about 80. The Friends Temperance Society was running, though no details were given. By 1903, the Adult School's Savings Club (a fairly common offshoot of these schools) held the mortgage on two properties. Eleven Friends were involved in the Friends Circulating Tract Association. By 1877, there were 14, engaged in fortnightly visits circulating the tracts, of which there were 28,000 by 1882, received by about 400 families. Most of these tracts were probably very short, simple documents of the sort produced by Hannah More earlier in the century. Some were actually referred to as leaflets. The only subjects specifically mentioned in the minutes were prayer, temperance, and the Yearly Meeting epistle. [19]

The Junior School, which would probably have been along the lines of the Charles Church Sunday School, was said to have come out of a regular gathering for Friends' and attenders' children arranged by Alfred P Balkwill. It may have started before the adult one, but whichever came first, there is no doubt that within a short while the Adult School was the more significant. In 1870 some members of Plymouth Meeting had thought that the junior school might be opened as a day school, but it was concluded that it would not qualify for a government grant and there would be other difficulties. In 1897, responding to a grant from the Preparative Meeting, the Junior School reported on its activities. It had started the year with 19 scholars and two teachers, and had just divided into junior and senior classes. Further divisions became necessary, made possible by help from a former pupil and two young men from the adult school, and by November in the same year, there were 50 children on the books, with an average attendance of 32. The school met in the afternoon.[20]

Meanwhile, there had been developments both externally and internally. Externally, Devon and Cornwall had come together in a single Quarterly Meeting. This had first been proposed in 1853, following a report from a committee set up by the Yearly Meeting to review the boundaries of Quarterly Meetings. Discussions had been held between Devon and Cornwall, but the matter was deferred, and nothing was done until the end of 1869. Between 1853 and 1869, of course, the railway through Plymouth had been extended into Cornwall, making travel much easier. In 12th month 1869, at a meeting at which women Friends were present, Devon received a minute from Cornwall Quarterly Meeting, where women Friends had also been present. The committee set up to meet with Cornwall, however, was all male. In the 4th month 1870, the report of the committee was received, and union was agreed, with the first united meeting being held in 10th month 1870 in Plymouth. For 1871, since Exeter had sold its Meeting House and was temporarily meeting in hired rooms, meetings were to be held at Liskeard, Plymouth, Falmouth and Plymouth again. The position of Plymouth Meeting had changed from being on the edge of a fairly small Quarterly Meeting to being in a central position in a fairly large one. It continued to be the largest meeting in the Quarterly Meeting. However, it was soon on its own in a Monthly Meeting, with Kingsbridge being discontinued in 1872 and Tavistock in 1873 (though not noted by the Quarterly Meeting till 1874). The task of looking after the buildings and burial grounds in Kingsbridge and Tavistock fell to Plymouth Friends, and occupied them from time to time.

At the end of that year of 1873, the Monthly Meeting had 131 members and 15 regular attenders, nearly all of whom would have been attached to Plymouth, out of 434 members and 86 attenders in the Quarterly Meeting as a whole. There had thus been some decline from the figure of 146 members in Plymouth Meeting in 1820. Considering that the town was continuing to expand rapidly, the comparative decline was much steeper. Where the occupations of Friends are given in the membership lists, they show that apart from four gentlemen, two-thirds of them were either commercial employers or self-employed professionals. The remainder included clerks and salesmen, skilled manual workers and unskilled manual workers. Most of these joined in the later part of the period, either through transfer or through convincement, probably through the adult school.[21]

In 1875 the Quarterly Meeting was enthused by a discussion at Yearly Meeting on the topic of "general meetings", that is to say a series of daily evangelising meetings within a selected area. A large committee was appointed to look into the matter. With no further ado, the committee organised a general meeting for the three towns of Plymouth, Devonport and Stonehouse in September of the same year, and they arranged for the Quarterly Meeting to be brought forward to coincide with it. Other Friends came from a distance to support it. The principal event at this, advertised separately from the others, was a public meeting at Plymouth Guildhall on Monday 20 September, entitled "War and its remedies from a Christian standpoint". The chair was taken by a Friend from Falmouth and the main speakers were from America. Over the period 17 – 21 September, there was a meeting at 11 each day except Saturday in the meeting house, and two to four meetings at a variety of locations in the three towns. The later report to Quarterly Meeting mentioned that meetings had also been held in outlying villages, but nothing was said about these in the press announcements. One paper reported fairly fully on the Guildhall meeting, without giving the attendance, and also reported briefly on a "largely attended" meeting at the Mechanics Institute in Plymouth, on the duty of Christian churches with regard to temperance. The report to Quarterly Meeting said that some of the meetings were large ones, and it was felt that notwithstanding some discouragements, there were really valuable and lasting results. But attendance by the public was "scanty", and it seems that for all the stir that Friends made, the bustling conurbation did not really notice.[22]

Around that same year, Plymouth Meeting started thinking about altering its Treville Street Meeting House again, though it did not finally decide on plans until 1882, when there was extensive remodelling. The walls remained, but there were alterations costing over £1000. During the alterations, which took over a year, meeting for worship was held in the schoolroom. The building was reopened in April 1883, and was described as more commodious. About 200 attended the opening, including "prominent townsmen" and Friends from Cornwall and other parts of Devon, it being the day after the Quarterly Meeting.[23]

Memories of this Meeting House were set down in writing in 1950 by Charles Reginald Fox: "On ascending a flight of steps you entered a small hall; on the left a waiting room, etc for men, and on the right a similar one for women. A doorkeeper stood at the entrance door of the Meeting Room and advised, with helpful suggestions to any visiting Friends, where to sit – most Plymouth Friends had their regular seats. I believe in earlier times men sat on the right side and women on the left, but this was before my time – families now all sit together. At the far end of the Meeting Room there were three large upright windows and a Gallery consisting of a long seat stretching the length of the wall with a rail in front. On one side sat the men – Ministers and Elders – and on the other side the women."[24]

The writer went on to a brief description of the course of a typical morning meeting, and mentions that those who lived in the country would be driven in by their coachmen who would then go off to their own places of worship. We also have an account of an evening meeting, and for what happened in the course of the meeting this is consistent with the description of the morning meeting. The account of the evening meeting is perhaps more revealing as coming from an outsider, James Thomas Rogers, who paid a visit in April 1888.

"Eliza and I visited for the first time in our lives a Quaker meeting House in Plymouth. The place was situated at the junction between Treville Street and Exeter Street, a square unpretentious building, there seemed to be a great number of small rooms visible from the vestibule, and at the back the large square meeting room, all plain and neat. A raised platform at the farther end with six divided seats at the back, and a rail in front, the service was notified on the board at the door to commence at 6.30, we got there in time, but found that Quakers do not make punctuality one of their special virtues, we were nearly alone for some minutes, but presently one and another dropped in, until, in about 15 minutes about 30 were in the room and the platform was occupied by 3 ladies and 3 gentlemen, without any peculiarities in dress, the colours were sober, but the dresses were not particularly antiquated, the bonnets being high fronted, a la mode, and one of them trimmed with what looked like flowers, the only female whom we saw with a Quaker bonnet on, was an old lady who sat in a side seat, not on the platform.

"About 6.45 a friend on the platform made a move to his knees (the rest mostly stood) and offered a prayer, lasting about 10 minutes, this was followed by another silence of about a quarter of an hour, when a man at the back stood up and gave an address, very halting, very deliberate, very ungrammatical, very dry, with a tinge of evangelism in it directed to the young people present – some 3 or 4 – then another long pause, after which one of the platform friends gave short address on the Lords Supper, in which he held that the actual celebration is not required, only that it should be done in spirit; a few more short speeches followed, then a prayer, another speech, short silence, then an old gentleman made a move, and all got up and marched out without benediction, the whole occupied less than an hour, and seemed tame and lifeless, no singing – some of the language used was very good, but there was a lack of fire, and very little argument, or logical reasoning, and we thought a very little of that sort of thing would go a long way with us."[25]

In 1873, the Monthly Meeting, in answering its Queries, had lamented that on First Day evenings and on weekdays, the time appointed for the meeting was "not well observed". Fifteen years later, it seems there had been no improvement. More generally, there had been a falling off in attendance at all meetings for worship, so that in 1883 the Monthly Meeting decided to send an address to those who did not attend.[26]

From 1860, the Yearly Meeting's guidance on marriages had been relaxed, and there had been other easings of expectations. This resulted in fewer disownments of wayward Friends but there were more resignations. Some of Charles Prideaux's family went to join the Plymouth Brethren, but probably more of those leaving went towards the established church. During much of this time, one of Plymouth's ministers, Helen Balkwill (granddaughter of Benjamin), was being given travelling minutes to enable her to travel in the ministry in various places from the outskirts of Plymouth to the west coast of America. But in 1880, having recently returned from Indiana, and sent in minutes from two Yearly Meetings there, she wrote from Reading to say that she had been baptised by immersion in September. Plymouth Monthly Meeting, which had also received a letter from her brother, Alfred P Balkwill, saying that he agreed with her views on baptism and the Supper, thought about it and asked her to retire from being a recorded minister. She submitted to the Monthly Meeting's views and was removed from the list of ministers. There was more prevarication over her brother, but a year later it was decided to take his letter as a resignation from being a recorded minister. He continued not only as a Quaker, but as a member of the Ministry and Oversight Meeting, and was given other jobs. Helen Balkwill not only remained in the Society of Friends, but on her marriage to (James) Rendel Harris, brought him into it as well. More on this later. In 1881 the Ministry and Oversight Meeting reported that "although a diversity of views respecting some important points of Christian Practice must still be acknowledged, it is satisfactory to believe that love prevails among us."[27]

Numbers were partly made up by convinced attenders joining. One of these, William Taylor, who applied at the end of 1876 and was accepted in 1877, caused the Monthly Meeting to hesitate because he was a worker in the (naval) Dockyard, though he pointed out that his job was nothing to do with fighting "more than any other firm". It continued to be the case that once accepted, members were entitled to help and support from the Meeting if they needed it, though this could not have applied to the curious case of two Swiss Friends accepted as members, apparently purely on account of the letter they had written, and "sympathy for them in their isolated position".[28]

Alongside the losses and gains within the three towns, there were also the transfers of membership to and from other parts of the country. Friends could be extraordinarily meticulous about these. In October 1889, Thomas Litten wrote from Leominster asking to be transferred to Herefordshire and Radnorshire Monthly Meeting. Some members of the Monthly Meeting wanted to know more about the circumstances in which he had left his previous job in Plymouth (where he seems to have been offered a partnership) and accepted one with the Home Mission Committee. There was a pernickety and increasingly irritated correspondence over this, and the matter was not settled until in January 1890 Thomas Litten came back to Plymouth to attend the Monthly Meeting, and even then the certificate may have been qualified. It appears that the difficulty (never stated in the letters) was that he had applied for membership only six months after starting to attend because he wanted the job with the Home Mission Committee; but it is also possible that obstacles were put in his way because the post of Home Missioner to which he had been appointed was controversial within the Society.[29]

As previously mentioned, Quaker evangelicalism tended to break down barriers with some other churches. In 1881 the Preparative Meeting happily sent representatives to an interdenominational committee set up to support the visit of the famous American evangelists Moody and Sankey. In 1895 the Monthly Meeting sent an address of welcome to the Wesleyan conference meeting in Plymouth, and in 1897 a similar address to the Baptist Union. Both were well received.[30]

From 1884 there were triennial reports,[31] which depict a great amount of activity, giving brief accounts (in very evangelical language) of the Adult School, the Mothers' Meeting, the Bible class on First Day evenings, the Friends Temperance Association, and the branch of the Missionary Helpers Union, which had the "special interest of young people". There was active involvement in the local Peace Association. For Friends' children, there were a Children's meeting held monthly, and Bible classes in a Friend's house on First Day afternoons. These reports did not mention the Pen and Pencil Society, a Friends' essay and sketching club, which started, probably, in the 1880s and in 1897 had a membership of 58 – it was probably thought too frivolous. Why frivolous? Earlier in the century, Friends would have mostly disapproved of poetry, but this society not only wrote about Tennyson and Longfellow, but they wrote verse of their own, including a comic poem about a young man who fooled Plymouth Quakers out of money and possessions, through his knowledge of Quaker ways and of some of their well-known names, and then went on to do the same in Exeter and Bristol. And many of the sketches were actually cartoons. The Society had an annual outing, but this was omitted in the 1896/97 session because of the Queen's Jubilee session.[32]

Plymouth's most conspicuous Quaker towards the end of the century and the beginning of the next was probably William Bray. Originating from St Blazey, he was educated at Sidcot School, which he reached by travelling by boat from Hayle. He came to Plymouth in 1857, working first as a tailor, than as a bank cashier, and eventually setting up in business with John Phillips as a forage merchant in Frankfort Street. He would have been 25 or 26 when the Adult School was set up in 1861, and was one of the first class-presidents. An ardent Liberal, he was elected to the Town Council for the Frankfort ward in 1887, and in 1893 became chairman of the Tramways committee. It was said that "the Corporation horses had in him a firm friend." He became an alderman in 1895, and also a JP. He had retired from business some years before his death in 1909, after some unspecified financial difficulties, but it is hard to see how he could have spent much time on his business. In addition to his council and magistrate duties, in which he was diligent, he was a founder of the Plymouth Co-operative Society, and President of the Total Abstinence Society, and had a heavy commitment to Friends, being an elder, overseer, secretary and treasurer of the Tract Association, a class-president in the Adult School, involved in most new initiatives, a property trustee, and treasurer of the Preparative Meeting for 20 years, overlapping with being clerk of the Monthly Meeting for 21 years, though he had asked to give up after 16. He was also in the Pen and Pencil Society, and among those who hosted its meetings. Such a level of activity could probably not have been maintained without the household who would have been employed as a matter of course. J F Winnicott, the Deputy Mayor, said of William Bray that he was a noble example of quiet patience and of love. He had never once seen a ruffle on his countenance, and it had been almost impossible to have anything but peace in his presence.[33]

The story of Plymouth Meeting has until this time been male-dominated. That is partly in the nature of the times – Quaker women had more organisational influence than those in other denominations – and partly in the nature of the records. But the longest and tenderest 19th century testimonies about deceased Friends are mostly for women. They include the two Sarah Abbotts already mentioned; Sarah Fox (died 1833, the widow of Francis), of whom it was said that her ministry was of an affectionate and persuasive character; and Elizabeth Prideaux (died 1856, the first wife of Charles Prideaux, both wives being called Elizabeth), whose testimony included extensive excerpts from the memoranda she made about her spiritual state, and whose funeral was attended by neighbours and the poor. In 1895, Sarah Anne Budge, very well known nationally in the Society and beyond for her writings on early Friends, came to live in Plymouth, but although she lived till 1905, she seems to have been in poor health much of the time and made little impact on the Meeting. [34]

Treville Street Meeting House

Adult School interior

57

Treville Street burial ground

Swarthmore (centre foreground) in the later 1920s

The new hall at Swarthmore

The lounge at Swarthmore

Chapter 5

World Wars and the Swarthmore Institute

In 1896 Plymouth Quaker Meeting entered on three major developments, each of which had probably been maturing for some time.

The first development was that the women's and men's business meetings combined. For many years the women had been joining the men whenever there was an important decision to be made. Now at the beginning of 1896 the Monthly Meeting agreed that the men and women's Preparative Meetings should meet jointly. At first the Monthly Meeting resisted having women come into its own meetings, but when, later in the year, the Yearly Meeting came out in favour of having joint sessions when appropriate, the resistance was in effect abandoned, and the Preparative Meeting began to appoint women representatives to the Monthly Meeting. In the Quarterly Meeting the resistance continued a little longer, with a decision that they would decide when joint sessions were appropriate, but in effect the merger went ahead. The women were soon being given jobs to do, though not usually in the finance field.[1]

In May 1896 Plymouth Friends acquired an additional Meeting House in Mutley. This was a small house which, when converted, provided seating for 47 people, plus those on the bench for ministers and elders. There was no central aisle, so the old division between men and women could not apply. The address given was 5 Ford Park, but the eastern boundary was the Plymouth Leat (often known as Drake's Leat), running alongside Mutley Plain. The address was soon changed to 62 Mutley Plain, and this was later renumbered to 72 Mutley Plain.[2]

The formal records do not tell us why this new centre was thought necessary; but when, in October 1904, a census was taken of attendance at Plymouth's Quaker meetings for worship, there was only an evening meeting in Mutley, and this may have been the case from the beginning. The attendance on those October First Day evenings varied between 22 and 29. This compares with Treville Street's 62 to 79 in the morning. (The evening meetings in Treville Street are not comparable, on account of the third development, to be described shortly.) Earlier in 1904 it had been agreed that the adult school could use the premises.[3]

The Friends who attended at Mutley did not form a separate Preparative Meeting, so there continued to be just one Preparative Meeting in the Monthly Meeting. Considering that they had an identical membership, it is surprising that on one occasion the Monthly Meeting partially overturned a recommendation of the Preparative Meeting. This was in connection with the third development.

At the end of 1896 the Preparative Meeting decided to introduce a formal address or Bible reading, along with hymn singing, into their First Day evening meetings for worship at Treville Street. There would still be a conventional Sunday evening meeting for worship at Mutley for those who did not want anything programmed. At the end of 1897, it was reported that the attendance had gone up from about 17 to about 60, but had then reduced to about 30, and that there were elements which were not very satisfactory. One was the quality of the hymn singing, and it was proposed to address this by introducing a portable musical instrument, on condition that it was removed afterwards every time. Another was that there was a need for the pastoral care of those attending. It may have been in order to remove this duty that it was proposed to stop calling it the Evening Meeting. The Monthly Meeting did not agree to this change of terminology, though it agreed to everything else, and the Quarterly Meeting also concurred. So at the very time that the Society of Friends nationally was beginning to move away from evangelicalism, Plymouth was going further into it.[4]

A large committee was appointed to look after the evening meeting. The surviving minutes of this committee (from 1902) show that the average attendance fluctuated considerably, going down from 70 to 38 and then up to 58. Most of those attending were not members, and most were associated with the Adult or Junior Schools. The committee appointed Friends to attend, but vocal ministry was not confined to them. The suggestion of hymns was apparently spontaneous, because complaints were made about the meeting being overburdened with hymns chosen at random. There was an Annual Tea for those who came. Around 1902, the evening meeting was preceded by "open air meetings" in front of the Meeting House in Treville Street, but although these probably attracted some increased attendance they seem to have lapsed fairly soon. In 1904 the committee appears to have tried to meet its obligations of oversight of those attending by keeping names and addresses with a view to regular visitation, but by the end of 1910 there was slackness in visiting non-attenders. The October 1904 census of attendance at meetings for worship shows the evening meeting attendance varying between 184 and 201, a figure which included children. In 1905 the children were split off from the main meeting, and a nationally known Friend was invited to launch the new arrangement. In fact there was a regular practice of having visiting speakers. In 1911, the regular attenders at the evening meeting were recognised through the new system of Associate Membership. There were soon 12 of these, but it seems the number was never large.[5]

Among the events of 1896, there were two separate applications for membership from residents at Princetown, whose letters of application referred merely to what they had read of Quaker beliefs. After visitation they were accepted. At more or less the same time, the meeting on Ministry and Oversight took notice of the fact that some Princetown residents had been meeting for worship after the manner of Friends. A small committee was appointed to look after that meeting. This arranged for a travelling minister who was visiting Plymouth to hold four meetings there over two days. It arranged for the Monthly Meeting to provide books and tracts, and for it to pay the rent of the Co-operative Rooms where the meeting was held. It also organised Friends to run weekday Bible readings followed by a meeting for worship. In 1898 the Monthly Meeting sought the help of the national Home Mission Committee to support the Princetown activity, and a woman Friend, Sarah Horstead, was found to live there for this purpose. At the end of 1900, by which time Monthly Meeting had taken over responsibility, Princetown meeting seemed to be thriving with attendances of 12 on First Day mornings and 38 in the evenings and a children's meeting of 48; but by the middle of the following year, with key people leaving the area and the Home Mission Committee withdrawing its support, the Princetown work was discontinued.[6]

In 1902 Plymouth Friends dealt with the absurdity of having two Meetings for church affairs with the same membership but the one overseeing the other. The Preparative Meeting could not be laid down because it owned (through trustees) both the Adult School and the Mutley meeting house. But its meetings were reduced to one a year, the only business being to receive a report from its finance committee. In 1931, after the buildings had been handed over to the Quarterly Meeting, permission was received for the Preparative Meeting to be completely discontinued.

At the time of the 1901 census, Plymouth's population had grown to 107,600 and Devonport to 70,400. The average number of people per house had reduced to just under eight in Plymouth, just under nine in Devonport and just under ten in Stonehouse. The membership of the Quaker Meeting had not matched the population increase, but still remained respectable. At some point in these years five members or former members from Plymouth found their way to Calgary in Canada, where there was an informal Quaker meeting which in 1915 sent its greetings to the Monthly Meeting.

It would be surprising if the evening meeting and the Adult School, with its ever-spreading commitments, together with the responsibilities for Kingsbridge's building and a certain amount of activity at Princetown did not occupy most of the energies of the Plymouth Quaker Meeting. Nevertheless it did pursue whatever the Yearly Meeting and the Quarterly Meeting asked it to pursue, on the slave trade, peace, Armenian relief, the licensing laws, and combatting militarism. There was a Friends Foreign Mission Association which had an annual meeting with a visiting speaker. In February 1905 Plymouth Friends called a meeting of clergy and "prominent citizens" to discuss betting and gambling. Held at the Athenaeum, there was an attendance of about 180, a committee was set up, and a petition was agreed asking for legislation on street gambling and on advertising.[7]

From 1906 there is a minute book for the Adult School, which now had a Council. At this time the Adult School had 214 men and 34 women in seven male and two female classes, with an average attendance during the year of 132 men and 34 women. Numbers had declined, with 173 leaving and only 125 joining. Classes seem to have started at 8.30 in the morning, and after they had begun entry was controlled by doorkeepers (separate ones for men and women). The school was governed by a Council with various officers and committees, including a school excursion treasurer, a magazine secretary, a librarian, a benevolent committee, a recreation room committee, and a lecturette committee. There were a Savings Bank for members, and a Coal and Goose club. When in 1905 the Monthly Meeting took up a collection for unemployed people, the money was channelled through the Adult School benevolent fund. The school was linked to local, regional and national networks, sent representatives to them, and had a scheme of intervisitation with other local schools. In 1908 the old movable organ was replaced by a proper pipe organ, accompanied by some controversy, as those who were enthusiastic about it had pressed ahead without proper authorisation. An old photograph shows it installed at the end of the main schoolroom. In 1912, when the detailed information from the

Council minute book comes to an end, there were 167 members and an average attendance of 102 in seven classes. Men outnumbered women by more than two to one, and only one of the classes was for women.[8] And then after this, the next mention that appears in the records is that in January 1918 the Monthly Meeting appointed a joint Adult and Junior School committee of only seven members. Clearly much had been changed, suddenly, by the war; but the Adult Schools, still segregated by gender, continued in some form even after the Treville Street premises had been abandoned, first at Lower Street Mission Hall then at Swarthmore.[9]

Around 1908 the Home Mission Committee appointed a worker, Ernest Dawe, to live and work in Devon and Cornwall. The Quarterly Meeting then set up an extension committee, of which he was the secretary. Among other activities this committee organised lecture schools once a year in conjunction with a Quarterly Meeting It was one of these events which saw the public return to Plymouth of (James) Rendel Harris. He was the son of a Plymouth house decorator, went from Plymouth Grammar School to Cambridge University, and had a distinguished international career as a palaeographer and biblical scholar. In 1880 he became a Quaker, on his marriage to the Helen Balkwill who has already been mentioned. Part of his career, from 1903, was as the first director of studies at Woodbrooke, the new Quaker college in Birmingham. Over the Easter period, 9th to 14th April 1914 he, with an American professor W. R. Rogers and a Quaker writer Elizabeth Fox Howard, held a lecture school in Plymouth. Unlike the "general meeting" it was very fully and favourably reported in the press, which gave surprisingly detailed accounts of such topics as the Babylonian and biblical flood, the "liturgy of the skylark" and the recent Moffatt translation of the Bible. This event, which took place just before the merger of the three towns of Plymouth, Devonport and Stonehouse, was the last lecture school to be organised on such a scale.[10]

The first world war broke out in August 1914 and immediately had an effect on Plymouth Meeting. Large numbers of troops came to Plymouth, taking over some schools, and it was agreed that the Education Authority could use the Adult School schoolroom to help out. That use had finished by early 1915 when the Education Authority paid for it with money provided by the War Office. The room was also used, on the initiative of some Friends, to provide a space for soldiers to write letters and read. The facility was continued until November 1915, after which it was said that the few remaining users would still find a welcome in the Adult School clubrooms. For a short period there had also been a Sunday evening "service" for the troops, but few had attended. The Meeting also responded to appeals for various funds, while 39 Friends, some of them elderly and infirm, responded to another appeal for unspecified help in connection with one of the funds. The Monthly Meeting considered the plight of German and Austrian citizens stranded in the town, and it was agreed to provide assistance to them, though in the end only six were identified and helped, four of whom had been on a liner that was captured and brought into Plymouth.[11]

Friends throughout the country were divided by the war, and the Yearly Meeting was unable to reach a position on what should be done. Some wanted to hold fast to the peace testimony and have nothing to do with the fighting. Others wanted to support the war, and many young members joined the armed forces. Yet others were willing to water down the peace testimony to the extent of participating in the Friends Ambulance Unit. From Plymouth at least two joined this, while another joined the 2nd Wessex Field Ambulance. None of this appears in the ordinary records. However, when conscription was introduced in January 1916, a special Yearly Meeting, called in that month, was able to unite. Conscription, after all, was an attack on freedom of conscience, and nearly all Friends would actively support freedom of conscience. Except in Plymouth. When West Devon Monthly Meeting received the Yearly Meeting statement they declined to do anything about it, and they even asked Falmouth Friends not to place it in the *Western Morning News* and *Western Daily Mercury*, as they had proposed to do. Plymouth Friends claimed they were not happy about some of the wording. They had, however, already established a committee to advise young men who were trying to decide what they should do, and they did visit conscientious objectors in the ordinary prison in Plymouth.[12] And when Quaker conscientious objectors at the Princetown Work Centre asked for their meeting to be recognised as an Allowed Meeting, this was agreed.

When conscription was introduced, those men who convinced tribunals that they were truly conscientious objectors were sent to Work Centres established by the Home Office. Dartmoor Prison was emptied of its normal prisoners to create one of these work centres, and it came into use in 1917. The majority of the C Os placed here did not have a religious motivation. One person who did have such a motivation (and later became a Quaker) wrote at the time that he had been "tossed into a mass of fairly intelligent men who viciously assail Christianity as being irrational." By May 1917, however, four Quakers, some attenders at Quaker meetings, and a few others had come together in a meeting for worship, and they wrote to West Devon Monthly Meeting (which of course consisted only of Friends attached to Plymouth Meeting) to ask for recognition as an Allowed Meeting. After investigations, the Monthly Meeting agreed to this. A minute book for the Allowed Meeting was started in 7th month 1917, and shows that these young men were doing their best to follow proper Quaker procedures within the constraints of the regulations to which they were subjected. However, they could not become a Preparative Meeting because they saw no point in transferring their membership to West Devon. The affairs of Princetown occupied the attention of the Monthly Meeting from time to time, and individual Friends, particularly those living out in that direction, gave some support. The Allowed Meeting was formally wound up in 4th month 1919.[13]

After receiving alarming reports on its financial situation, the Monthly Meeting decided in September 1916 that it could no longer afford to keep on running two Meeting Houses, that both Treville Street and the new premises in Mutley should be sold off, and that a new Meeting House should be acquired in Mutley. Mutley was a preferred location because most members now lived to the north of the town. There had always been Friends from surrounding areas, but whereas in the early days they seem to have been mostly to the east, they now tended to be in the north, either in the suburbs or further out on the fringes of Dartmoor. In addition Treville Street seemed to give continual problems, the most recent being a worry over sanitation. The Adult School building, though this was not mentioned at the time, was to be included in the sale. The permission of the Quarterly Meeting was obtained for the sale of Treville Street, and also for the sale of Kingsbridge Meeting House, though not the burial ground and garden, the proceeds to be applied to the new building. No permission was needed for the sale of the existing premises at Mutley or the Adult School, both of which were owned by the Preparative Meeting. In the event the garden alongside the Meeting House was retained and numbered as 74.

Then, without any building having been sold, the new building committee recorded on 10 May 1917 that 76 & 78 Mutley Plain, two semi-detached villas, had been acquired at a cost of £2600 (£100 more than the committee had previously specified as the maximum). In September there were plans for the adaptation of the building, at an estimated cost of £100, and on 31 January 1918 the first Meeting for Worship was held there, on the occasion of the Devon and Cornwall Quarterly Meeting being held in Plymouth. The other buildings were sold in the course of 1918, and more than covered the cost of the new acquisition, even after the repayment of a mortgage, though Kingsbridge only raised £290 less expenses. The burial ground remained in Friends' ownership, though in 1911 the Quakers had obtained the allocation of ground in Eggbuckland (now Efford) cemetery. In 1926 the Treville Street burial ground was closed to further burials. The library and some furniture were transferred from Treville Street. As the library room upstairs was little used, a bookcase with those books most likely to be borrowed was placed in the porch.[14]

At first the Quakers occupied only 76 Mutley Plain, with a tenant remaining in 78. The first clear origins of the new adult education work that was soon associated with the new building were in December 1918 when the meeting of overseers asked the finance committee to give notice to that tenant, in order to give room for development work, though it seems that they did not have anything specific in mind. Their minute said, among other things, "We are reminded that we are often apt to be kept back by dwelling too much on our own limitations instead of taking hold of the Power which should be our strength and inspiration."[15]

In July of the following year the clerk to overseers, (George) Rendel Harris called a special meeting of overseers to lay a concern before them. It was known that a Friend called Edwin Gilbert, who seems to have been involved in post-war relief work, was intending to spend some months in the west of England. It was agreed that he should be asked to live in the upper part of 78 Mutley Plain in order to assist with development work, and the proposal was also agreed by the Monthly Meeting. Gilbert came, met Plymouth Friends, and agreed to take up residence. It seems to have been his drive, together with the efforts of the extension committee, which really got the work going. Early in 1921 Rendel Harris resigned as clerk to overseers because of the amount of work he had as secretary of the extension committee, which had the main responsibility for the activities. Another Friend specifically mentioned as playing a significant part in getting Swarthmore going was Charles A Goodbody, who had moved to Plymouth for his health in the 1890s.[16]

At the end of 1919 a long hut was bought and erected on the north side of the building. This was the original Swarthmore Hall. There was a formal opening on Monday 8 March 1920, when the headmaster of Plymouth College gave an address on the master works of English poetry. The activities were intended for adults, but as a social venue it was besieged by lads of 15 to 18 , so in 1920 a second hut was erected alongside Ford Park Lane at the back of the building, and labelled as a billiard room, under the name of the Forty Club.[17]

When Edwin Gilbert left early in 1922, John and Blanche Ridges were appointed as wardens. John had been the third headmaster of Leighton Park, Reading, the new Quaker boarding school for the academically able, and Blanche had also been a considerable figure in the school. Unfortunately Blanche died in December and John was too distressed to continue without her, so it was decided to appoint another couple as wardens. After soundings had been taken, Arthur Gage and his wife Enid were appointed in 1923. They soon began to play active roles in the Monthly Meeting, in addition to their work.[18]

There are no formal records of the work of Swarthmore before 1926, but in March 1921, while Edwin Gilbert was still there, an article appeared in the Quaker periodical *Workers at Home and Abroad*, which spoke of the social, educational and religious aspects of the work. It said that the Workers Educational Association had accepted with alacrity an invitation to use the hall, and were holding weekly lectures. There was a library of 1300 volumes. In November 1923 a short item appeared in the *Western Morning News*. This mentioned groups on elocution, geography and world power; a dramatic society, an orchestra and glee party; a WEA class in English Literature; two study circles; an ambulance class; general lectures on Wednesday evenings; men's and women's adult schools on Sundays; and a library, reading room and billiard room. The Hall was the scene of a Sunday evening "fellowship" meeting, which followed on from a brief conventional Meeting for Worship in the Meeting House and included hymn singing. Swarthmore Hall's overall aim was said to be to foster the spirit of fellowship. It seems that even in the early stages Swarthmore differed from previous work in this field in that there was active co-operation with the W E A, with university extension courses, and with the local education authority.

From 1920 the Monthly Meeting extension committee, which ran the institute, was allowed to co-opt non-members, provided that its executive committee consisted only of Quakers. But in May 1927 Swarthmore the Monthly Meeting agreed Swarthmore should have a proper Council, with representatives of the groups engaged in it. Soon afterwards it was also agreed that Swarthmore should have its own bank account, though its finances did not permit that to happen for a while. There were by this time lecture courses, handicrafts, and a football team, in addition to what had been happening in 1923 . It was affiliated to the Educational Settlements Association, which made it a grant. The 1937 appeal for an extension contained an even longer list of activities.[19]

Meanwhile the overseers had again approached the Monthly Meeting at the beginning of 1924. In their minute they said that "We have been favoured by a vocal ministry which has drawn, kept, and built up our membership," and they went on to suggest that the time had come to take steps for the provision of a larger Meeting House. The Monthly Meeting agreed, a committee was appointed, and two alternative plans were drawn up for a meeting house to be built on the south side of the building, but projecting to the west as far as Ford Park Lane. When the Quarterly Meeting was asked for help with funding, it agreed to provide £500 for a meeting house to accommodate 120 Friends, but £750 for a scheme to take 180 Friends, with additional lavatory accommodation. The larger scheme was adopted. Money was raised, and during the work the meeting for worship was held in makeshift rooms. The construction required a low level (up to 20 feet in height) extension and rearrangement on the south and west sides of the building. The entrance was set back from the line of the front of the building, so that from Mutley Plain the building still had just the two gable ends of the two villas, with the Meeting House appended onto the south-west corner, while the north end of the building was dominated by the very large, long hut projecting from alongside the building nearly as far as the pavement. The entrance to the Meeting House opened onto a lobby with cloakrooms on the left, and then there were steps down to the meeting room.[20]

The first meeting for worship in the new accommodation was held on 13th December 1925. The confident Friends who had recommended the development were not to know that as far as nominal membership numbers were concerned, Plymouth Meeting had reached its peak in 1923 with 164 members. This included children, and members in other parts of the country and abroad. Thereafter there was a slow, erratic decline, with small increases in some years. Thirty years later, in 1952, the number was down to 109 . All the activity left the Meeting with an overdraft, which was exacerbated by repairs and the maintenance of the Treville Street burial ground, and at the end of 1929 had grown to over £630. This took some time to reduce, but forty years later the Meeting was again a prosperous one.[21]

But for now Plymouth Meeting was thriving. At the end of 1925 a report to the Quarterly Meeting mentioned the adult school, week-end schools "to several of which we have been indebted for more intensive work than is possible in single lectures", and Young Friends having occasional special meetings. It would appear that the Young Friends group was especially lively. In the summer of 1927, a group of nine of them paid a visit to Exeter and later to a special meeting at Spiceland. They were accompanied by senior Quakers, but when Exeter Preparative Meeting wrote a minute of thanks it was the Young Friends who were particularly thanked for the encouragement they had given.[22]

Plymouth did not have the severe and chronic unemployment which afflicted communities in some other parts of the country at this time, but it had been bad enough for the Monthly Meeting to have discussions on the subject, with occasional collections for the Mayor's Fund for the unemployed. However, the successful scheme for allotments for the unemployed which Friends started and maintained in Plymouth came not from local initiative but from the national Quaker project. In December 1931 an organiser, Richard

Cottam, arrived in Plymouth, and in a whirl of activity met with various key people, attended the Monthly Meeting, arranged a meeting of Quakers and others to set up a committee, produced a leaflet to be handed to unemployed benefit claimants, got the Council's allotments committee to discuss the scheme, and had disappeared by the end of the month. The leaflet he had printed offered seed potatoes, seeds, fertiliser etc at about one quarter of the shop price, with the facility to pay in weekly instalments. The Council offered 91 allotments to the committee he had left behind, its secretary being Arthur Gage.[23]

By June 1932 Gage was able to report to the committee that 130 men had been accepted onto the scheme, of whom 79 had had allotments in the previous year and 51 were new. Two tons eight hundredweight of seed potatoes had been handed out, two tons 14 hundredweight of lime, with seeds, bags of fertiliser, spades, forks, hoes, rakes and mattocks in commensurate quantities. The original consultation had decided not to hold a public meeting, but in November 1932 the Monthly Meeting asked its Home Service Committee to arrange one, with a speaker from the central offices. When reported in the local press, the emphasis was on the appeal made by the local MP, Sir Francis Dyke Acland, for landowners to make unused land available. He praised the way the scheme was "encouraging self help by unemployed men in a way which will give them occupation, interest, help and extra food . . . . to a better degree than under any other scheme hitherto devised." He gave credit to the Society of Friends and announced that the government would be matching the money it raised. A different organiser from the Friends central allotments committee, John Robson, said that it was more than a cheap seed scheme because it got unemployed men together. There were also contributions from the chairmen of the council allotments committee and the Plymouth and District Allotments Association.[24]

The scheme grew in succeeding years, and by the end of the 1933 season it had spread to Tavistock, Saltash, Shaugh Prior and other places. Presumably because of Arthur Gage's involvement, it came to be considered as a Swarthmore scheme. In 1933 two Friends were appointed to support him in the administration of the Swarthmore Allotment Holders Association. In 1934 there was a well attended series of lectures given to the allotment holders, by two lecturers, one of them a Ministry of Agriculture horticultural adviser, probably recruited through Francis Lawson. In 1935 there were 418 beneficiaries, slightly down on the year before.[25]

March 1935 saw a proposal for major alterations to the Swarthmore building. This was agreed in general terms, and was followed by discussions. Work actually started in 1937 and continued to 1939. It resulted in the Mutley Plain frontage to which people became accustomed in post-war years, with the three gable ends and a single front entrance in the central one. The hut, the original Hall, was demolished, a hall with a stage occupied much the same space as the Meeting House, and a new, smaller Meeting House was constructed within the building.[26]

In 1938 the Monthly Meeting set up a small committee to help refugees, mostly from Germany and central Europe. The numbers it helped may have been small, but the work involved was substantial. They were in touch with over 100 refugees and gave material assistance to over half. This required getting to understand the various regulations that applied; co-ordinating with national and regional bodies; working with the Lord Mayor's committee; finding accommodation and work, education or training; matching refugees to placements then sometimes moving them to better ones; finding guarantors; raising money; arranging free dentistry; starting an international club; rescuing luggage from the docks, where there was pilfering; and so on. Once the war started, there was the problem that German refugees in sensitive areas such as Plymouth were liable to internment. They could be moved to "safe" areas, but there was difficulty both in finding out where these were, and in finding work there.[27]

For the Meeting, the second world war did not bring the divisions of the first. When, just before the war, the government introduced a Military Training Bill, the Monthly Meeting not only ordered 500 copies of the Meeting for Sufferings statement on it, but appended to it their own statement offering help to young men who thought they might be affected by it. A small committee was set up for this purpose. At the end of 1940, the Women's Free Church Council (in which Friends were already playing an active part) invited Friends to nominate a future president. The Monthly Meeting first enquired whether they were aware of Friends' views on war (they were) before nominating Enid Gage, who enjoyed a very successful year of office.[28]

In 1945, Plymouth Quakers agreed on a minute setting out what had happened to the Meeting and its members during the Second World War. This says much that did not go into the month to month records.

At the beginning of the war the work of extending and adapting the building to improve the adult education facilities was coming to an end, and in 1940 a grant was successfully claimed from the Ministry of Education. Some things went on as normal. The minute records that during the bombing raids, the building was only hit once, when the roof was damaged by incendiary bombs. Two Meetings for Worship continued to be held each Sunday, though after the heavy raids of 1941 the evening meeting was changed to the afternoon for a time. When it went back to the evening, an afternoon meeting was held once a month "to help meet the needs of Friends residing at a distance". These had been having serious difficulties with transport.

There were no fatal casualties among Quakers as a direct result of the raids. Eight businesses associated with Quakers had their premises destroyed. Some children were evacuated to the USA or Canada, and some families with young children moved out of town.

Ten men and one woman were registered as conscientious

objectors. Most were granted only conditional exemption, dependent on their occupation. One of these joined the Friends Ambulance Unit, but five others who were presumably not liable for military service also joined either the Friends Ambulance Unit or the Friends Relief Service. Three people from Plymouth not connected with Quakers also joined the F A U. Nine men served with the armed forces. Advice was given to conscientious objectors facing tribunals or experiencing other problems.

However, it looks as though the greatest impact on the life of the Meeting came from the building functioning as what was called a Rest Centre. This helped people made homeless by the air raids. The City Council provided beds, bedding, equipment and medical supplies. The building was staffed by 18 members of the Meeting and members of St John Ambulance Nursing Division. During the raids of March and April 1941, when the Rest Centre was open day and night, there was also support from a contingent of the Friends Ambulance Unit. A War Victims Relief Committee gave other help to people passing through the Centre. The minute records: "The horror of the nights of March and April 1941 will ever remain to us a fitting commentary on the futility and tragedy of modern warfare. Night after night, homeless citizens, bewildered, fearful and distraught, came or were brought to Swarthmore. All rooms including the Hall and (at times) the Meeting House were used to accommodate them. Evening by evening they were removed to outlying districts to clear the premises for anticipated raids of the coming night. Pitiful were many of the stories to which we listened in those days." The building was also used for meetings of refugees from the Channel Islands. The minute does not mention that the Monthly Meeting gave permission for the Unitarians, whose premises had been destroyed, to use the building, though this seems not to have been taken up.

Swarthmore Settlement continued functioning as an adult education centre throughout this time, and even extended its activities. It added First Aid and Home Nursing classes to its original selection.

Chamber concerts and plays were put on. One concert was held by candlelight. This was after the roof had been damaged and the lighting system was not working. Because other buildings had been destroyed, Swarthmore was used for events for which it would not normally have been considered, including royal visits.

The minute also mentions the two hostels with which Plymouth Friends were involved. Both these were run by the Friends Relief Service. The Brent Moor House hostel housed 16 children from the Hartley House school for the deaf in Plymouth, with their three teachers. It had five FRS staff, two of whom were from Plymouth. The hostel at Skisdon, St Kew, Cornwall, was for elderly and infirm evacuees. Like Brent Moor House, it suffered from its remoteness, but a link with Plymouth Friends was maintained. The Plymouth Friend who was the warden, Lilian Piper, maintained that the hostel was meeting a peacetime need as well as a wartime one, but after looking into it, Friends concluded that there was insuperable difficulty in raising money to continue the work.[29]

After the war, with many of the city centre shops destroyed, Mutley Plain had a new importance as a shopping centre, and Friends received enquiries about selling off its land at 74. The Meeting did not agree to this, but did agree to let part of the land and permit the setting up of a temporary building for a shop displaced from further down the road. It refused a later application for the other part of the land.[30]

In 1948 Donald Bentley in effect took over as warden of Swarthmore, Arthur Gage being seriously ill. Donald Bentley made his own place in the affections of Plymouth Friends, and among the posts he took on was that of Prison Minister at Dartmoor. The amount of work was such that a second Prison Minister had to be appointed, and the difficulties of transport at these times were such that both of them were dependent on a lift by two other members who had cars.[31]

The Treville Street burial ground had been closed to further burials in 1925. In July 1955 the Corporation notified the Monthly Meeting of its intention to issue a compulsory purchase order for it. This was in order to construct the roundabout around Charles Church. Agreement was reached on a price, on the assignment of a spot in Efford cemetery which the Monthly Meeting would own for the scattering of ashes, and on the reburial of the human remains in a common grave. In November a notice appeared in the press, and Mr W H Wingate, an expert on William Cookworthy, expostulated about the common grave. He gathered to his support the Curator of the City Museum, the general managers of the Bristol Pottery and Balkwill & co, the firm started by Cookworthy; and he raised over £300 for a separate burial for his remains. The Monthly Meeting relented and agreed that the remains should be buried separately, at their expense. The money that had been raised was put towards an annual Cookworthy Prize for the best ceramics student at the College of Art. The Corporation was dilatory in paying the purchase price for the burial ground, and had to be taken to court before the money was finally received in May 1963.[32]

In 1954 a new constitution was approved for Swarthmore, taking it a further step towards being totally independent of Plymouth Meeting; but for the moment the life of the Meeting and the activities at Swarthmore were still very much intertwined. There was a lot of social activity, involving the children as well as the adults. Around this time between 14 and 24 members were attending Monthly Meeting. As for the meetings for worship, it seems that at some point hymn singing had spread from the evening meetings to the main meeting in the morning. A hymn could be requested and if someone was available to play the piano, it would be sung. This did not please everyone, but as late as 1960 the Monthly Meeting bought new hymn books. The last hymn is said to have been sung in Plymouth Meeting in 1965.[33]

At the beginning of 1951 the Monthly Meeting agreed to an

Allowed Meeting in Tavistock, though it was only monthly. It ended in September 1954, but in January 1956 a Meeting started in Salcombe, and was given Allowed status in April. Monthly Meeting accepted invitations to meet in Salcombe in November 1968 and again in February 1970. Plymouth Meeting was no longer isolated as a Quaker community in west Devon.

Whatever the accounts of happy children's classes, the tendency was for those children not to continue with Friends. The newcomers who partially replaced them were mostly paid professionals, and not the sort of business person who had been the backbone of the Meeting. In 1969 the nominal membership was 96, with 24 attenders. The Meeting's decline in activity and numbers was after that occasionally checked by short-lived initiatives, but none on the same scale as before.

Appendix 1

Plymouth Monthly Meeting minutes on marriage procedures

<u>17th 7th month 1676</u>

The forme of a Certificate for Marriages

Whereas AB of &c and CD of &c having laid theire Intentions of Mariage before severall publick Meeteings of the people of god called Quakers in &c which was approved of &c, now this is to Certifie all people whome it may concern that for the full determining of the Intentions a fore sayd this 1st day 5 mo in the year according to the account now used in England one thousand six hundred seventy six in an Assembly of the afore sayd people & others at &c, the sayd AB did sollemnly in the feare of god according to the example of the holy men of god recorded in the Scriptures of truth, take this sayd CD to be his wife, and she the sayd CD did then and there in like manner take the sayd AB to be her husband, each of them promising to bee faithfull one to the other and we who were present at there taking each other have heare unto sett our hands witnessing unto the same this day & yeare a fore sayd.

Record of Marrages

AB: of &c Grocer the / day of the : in the year 1676 in an Assembly of the people of god called Q: at Plymouth did sollemnly in the feare of god take CD: of &c to be his wife & the sayd CD did then and there take the sayd AB: to be her husband each of them promiseing to be faithfull one to the other so long as they should live, in the presence of &c.

Upon the debate about the order of the proseedings of all Mariages it was Concluded, one, that the persons intending to take one another as man and wife shall gooe both the man & also the woman, & lay before the womens Meeting their Intentions, & then that two: of the women of the said meeteing shall come forth to the men's next Monthly Meeteing & bring in their Sence & Judgment how they find them in clearness, & soo to be there upon referred to the Judgment of the monthly meeteing – whether to: be allowed or not.

Appendix 2

Testimony concerning Francis Fox

"The memory of the Just is blessed." Under an apprehension that religious advantage is often derived to posterity in holding up to view the character of the righteous, when their services in the Militant Church are brought to a peaceful conclusion, we are induced to give forth the following Testimony concerning our beloved Friend Francis Fox of Plymouth who departed this life the 18th of the 9th month 1812 and was interred in Friends' Burying Ground there the 25th of the same, aged 46 years and a Minister about 15 years. An unusual number of persons of various denominations testified their respect for the deceased by attending the burial.

In taking a view of him in his approach toward manhood, a time of life when many are carried away by the allurements of the World, we shall find him wisely choosing the paths of virtue, and by taking heed to that Word "which was a lamp to his feet and a light to his path", he was preserved in a good degree of innocency; yet he has been known to acknowledge that he was at one time drawn so far aside as to alter his apparel something nearer the fashion of the times. This he found opened a door to greater trials than he was first aware of, in being joined by those whose company and conversation brought a burthen to his mind, after which he became willing to submit to that simplicity in external appearance which he conceived became a disciple of a crucified Lord.

At an early age he became qualified for an Elder in the church, thereby verifying the observation that "Honourable age is not that which standeth in length of time, nor that which is measured by number of years, but wisdom is the grey hair unto Man, and an unspotted life is old age."

He not only preached by example, but had a precious gift in the ministry committed to him, in the exercise of which his appearances were lively, convincing and clear; accompanied by a beautiful simplicity and great humility of mind.

In him the Christian character shone with peculiar brightness, evincing that true religion, which operates by purifying the heart, necessarily produces works of righteousness – The prominent features of his mind were, love to God, and goodwill to Man. Under this sacred influence he proved a disciple of Him who "went about doing good". Deeply interested in things connected with the welfare of his fellow creatures, he was a liberal & zealous promoter of public works of benevolence: to the poor and wretched of every description he was an unwearied but unostentatious benefactor, and justly attributing many of the evils which exist in this class of society, to the want of right instruction in early life, he was earnestly and successfully engaged in extending this blessing to the poor children of his native town.

In the midst of this career of usefulness it has pleased unsearchable Wisdom to take him from us. May the contemplation of his virtues & the loss sustained by society stimulate others to pursue the same to pursue the same Christian course and thus shew forth the efficacy of a religion that produces such excellent fruits, and which if it operated on the hearts and conduct of mankind generally, would more extensively manifest a state of things consonant with the angelic anthem "Glory to God in the highest, and on earth, peace, goodwill towards men".

That a life so devoted to the service of his Creator and his fellow creatures should close in peace, might have been expected, and of which we have no doubt; for although he did not appear to apprehend his end so near, nor express much on the subject, yet the sweetness of spirit that attended him in his illness seemed to imply that his peace was seated, and that he had only to wait the summons to be removed from Time to the inheritance of a glorious immortality with the saints in light.

Signed by 21 men and 25 women

(Use of capitals partly modernised)

Notes

Abbreviations used:

MM minutes(+ date): Minute books of Plymouth Monthly Meeting, *or* Plymouth and Kingsbridge Monthly Meeting, *or* Western Division of Devon(shire) Monthly Meeting, held at PWDRO

QM minutes (+ date): Minute books of Devon Quarterly Meeting *or* Devon and Cornwall Quarterly Meeting, held at PWDRO.

PM minutes (+ date) Minute books of Plymouth Preparative Meeting (unless otherwise specified), held at PWDRO

Besse, *Sufferings*: Besse, Joseph. *A Collection of the Sufferings of the people called Quakers for the Testimony of a Good Conscience.* Printed and sold by Luke Hinde. 1753. pp 151 onwards.

Braithwaite, *Beginnings:* Braithwaite, William C. *The Beginnings of Quakerism.* 2nd edition prepared by Henry J Cadbury. Cambridge University Press. 1970.

Braithwaite, *Second Period:* Braithwaite, William C. *The Second Period of Quakerism.* Second edition prepared by Henry J. Cadbury. Cambridge University Press. 1961

Dymond: Dymond, Francis W. (Devon and Cornwall Quarterly Meeting) *Trust Property within the County of Devon.* Published for private circulation. 1899. Copy in PWDRO

PWDRO: Plymouth and West Devon Record Office

Selleck (History 1): Selleck, A.D. *Plymouth Friends: A Quaker History.* Transactions of the Devonshire Association, vol 98. 1966.

87

Selleck (History 2): Selleck, A.D. *Plymouth Friends: A Quaker History, Part II.* Transactions of the Devonshire Association, vol 99. 1967

The two articles above printed together in a single volume.

Selleck (JFHS): Selleck, A.D. *The Trial of Thomas Salthouse and Miles Halhead.* Journal of the Friends Historical Society, vol 49, no 3. 1960

Selleck (*Cookworthy*): Selleck, A.D. *Cookworthy: "A man of no common clay"* (alternative title: *Cookworthy 1705 – 80 and his circle*). Barron Jay. 1978

Sewel, *History*: Sewel, William. *The History of the Rise, Increase and Progress of the Christian People called Quakers.* Printed and sold by James Phillips and Son. 1799.

Worth: R N Worth. *The History of Plymouth.* 2nd edition. W B Brendon & Son. 1873.

Names of days and months

For much of the time covered by this history, Quakers would not use the common names for months and days of the week, because these names were derived from those of heathen gods. Instead they used numbers, with Sunday being called First Day. In the early years, during the slow and confused changeover from having the year start on 25 March to the new system of having it start on 1 January, there can be uncertainty as to whether First Month refers to January or March, and so on. Usually, however, it would have been March. This changed in 1752 when Friends complied with the new law starting the year on 1 January, and from then on, First Month was definitely January. Occasionally Plymouth Quakers would refer to a date between January and March by referring to both the years, e.g. 1676/7.

Notes on chapter 1. Beginnings

1. See Glossary

2. For the Quaker system of dating, see the note above.

3. MM minutes under 1680, reproduced in *First Publishers of Truth*, ed Norman Penney. Headley Brothers. 1907. For the use of First Day for Sunday, see note on names of days and months, above. For the use of the word "testimony", see Glossary.

4. MM minutes, under 1680, reproduced in *First Publishers of Truth*, ed Norman Penney. Headley Brothers. 1907.

5. *The Wounds of an Enemie in the House of a Freind*, probably by Thomas Salthouse. Printed for Giles Calvert. 1656. Ganniecliffe's name and the location of John Harris's house are taken from George Brookes's deposition, quoted in Selleck (JFHS).

6. Norman Penney, ed. *Extracts from State Papers*. Headley Brothers. 1913. The information on Hatsell (who acquired the Saltram estate around this time) is taken from the Oxford Dictionary of National Biography. The naval agent was the representative of the Navy Board, which supervised the administration of the navy.

7. *The Wounds of an Enemie in the House of a Freind,* as above

8. *A short account of the Barbarous sufferings of Margaret Killam, Priscilla Cotten, Mary Cole and Barbara Pattison, by the Government of the Town of Plymouth* . . . , printed as part of the pamphlet *The West Answering to the North in the fierce and cruel persecution of the Son of God, As appears in the following short relation of the unheard of and inhuman sufferings of Geo. Fox, Edw. Pyot and William Salt at Launceston . . . and of one and twenty men and women taken up in a few days in the high ways of Devon.* Printed for

Giles Calvert. 1657 The pamphlet issued by Killam and Pattison was also published by Giles Calvert, 1656. Thomas Martin is not given as vicar of Charles Church until 1690, so he may have been a curate. Margaret Killam's origins are given in Richard Hoare's *Balby Beginnings: The launching of Quakerism* (Balby Monthly Meeting. 2002)

9. Braithwaite *Beginnings*

10. *A short account of the Barbarous sufferings of Margaret Killam, Priscilla Cotten, Mary Cole and Barbara Pattison*, as above. This states that the oath was administered by the Mayor, John Page, and other magistrates, but Justinian Peard seems to have been the Mayor at this time (Worth), though John Page would still have been a Justice of the Peace. The pamphlet is mentioned in Rosemary Moore's *The Light in their Consciences: The early Quakers in Britain 1646 – 1666* (Pennsylvania State University Press. 2000). It was printed by Giles Calvert, the Quakers' usual printer for their approved publications.

11. Selleck (JFHS)

12. Budge, Frances Anne. *Miles Hallhead and Thomas Salthouse*. Friends Quarterly Examiner, vols 20 and 21, 1886 & 1887

13. Dymond.

14. Letter from Priscilla Cotton to Margaret Fell, in Swarthmoor Manuscripts, Friends House Library, quoted in Selleck (History 1).

Notes on chapter 2, Organisation and persecution

1. Besse, *Sufferings.*

2. Besse, *Sufferings*

3. Braithwaite, *Second Period.*

4. MM minutes 12th month 1671

5. Dymond; for the different names of the street, see the maps of Plymouth dated 1620, 1765 and 1830 in PWDRO; the list of contributors is in the Monthly Meeting minute book from 1669: paper at the end of the book; 8th month 1678 Katharine Martindale to have the chamber over Peter Rowe's rent free; 5th month 1681, and account books into 19th century.

6. MM minutes 4th month 1674

7. MM minutes 2nd month 1674. Matthew Crooker's name is always so spelt in the minute book, but he may have been one of the Croker family of Lyneham.

8. MM minutes 6th month 1680 and 3rd month 1695. Matthew Crooker was again present at Monthly Meeting in 9th month 1696

9. QM minutes 6th month 1677

10. MM minutes 7th month 1676

11. Letter from Kingsbridge dated 11th month 1678 copied into the MM minute book.

12. Besse, *Sufferings.* The detail about Richard Samble being on his

knees in prayer was given by Sewel, *History*, who also mentioned that the excrements were thrown on them out of a window.

13. Besse, *Sufferings*.

14. Sewel, (*History 1*). A shorter version of the petition, omitting the information given about Plymouth serge-makers, is given in Besse, *Sufferings*. The original of the petition does not appear to have survived in Quaker records.

15. Selleck (History 1).

16. MM minutes 5th month 1689

Notes on chapter 3: the eighteenth century

1. MM minutes 1st month 1757

2. MM minutes 11th month 1739

3. Testimony to Sarah Abbott in MM minutes 1803

4. MM minutes 12th month 1697 and 5th month 1699

5. MM minutes 7th month1690, and PM minutes 12th Month 1791

6. MM minutes 1743 and 8th month 1736

7. MM minutes 3rd month 1767 mention that there should now be a Select Monthly Meeting for Ministers and Elders to match the Quarterly Meeting one

8. MM minutes 12th month 1770

9. MM minutes 1687 and 7th month 1691 and Dymond

10. MM minutes 5th month 1695 to 5th month 1696

11. Dymond

12. MM minutes 9th month 1696; Dymond and MM minutes 5th month 1722; MM minutes 6th month 1736

13. MM minutes 11th month 1722 to 2nd month 1723

14. MM minutes 10th month 1768

15. Fox, Hubert. *The Story of William Cookworthy*. Cookworthy Museum. 1972

16. MM minutes 10th and 11the month, 1735

17. MM minutes 1st and 2nd month 1745

18. MM minutes 9th month 1742, QM minutes 10th month 1742 and 8th month 1743, and Selleck (*Cookworthy*), which gives more background.

19. Testimony to William Cookworthy in MM minutes 3rd month 1781, and Oxford Dictionary of National Biography – this does not compartmentalise Cookworthy's life as much as some biographies, and makes it easier to follow the chronology.

20. N.A.M. Rodger (*The Wooden World*. William Collins. 1986) argues that conditions in the Navy were more attractive than in the merchant ships.

21. Worth, pp 263 – 268. The effect of the town's over-dependence

on the prize goods trade was seen after the end of the war in 1815 when Plymouth's prosperity abruptly declined.

22. QM minutes 11 month 1746

23. MM minutes 7th month 1747 (the second meeting that month), QM minutes 8th month 1747. Yearly Meeting minutes 1748. Selleck (*Cookworthy*) quotes letters from Cookworthy in which he mentions both a local and a London Quaker involved in such dealing, and voices his frustration.

24. MM minutes 10th month 1747

25. Stagg, R. *Friends' Queries and General Advices1682 – 1860*. Journal of the Friends Historical Society., vol 49, no.4. 1961); MM minutes 12th month 1807 and 1st month 1808. The issue seems to have faded from view. It is not possible to find out the Gracechurch Street side because the minutes from this period were destroyed in 1821.

26. MM minutes 3rd month 1781

27. MM minutes 7 month 1758, 2nd and 3rd month 1759, 6th month 1768 to 6th month 1771; disciplinary papers in PWDRO.

28. For the role of the Women's Meeting, see, e.g., Women's Meeting minutes 5th month 1765, 4th month 1768 to 7th month 1770. For Anne Price: disciplinary papers in PWDRO. The letter is actually dated 1st month 1774, but as it is not dealt with until 2nd month 1775, it seems likely that the writer simply got the year wrong.

29. Letter in disciplinary documents in PWDRO, MM minutes 6th month 1780 and 5th month 1781.

30. Information on C W Dymond from James Gregory.

Correspondence etc relating to interment of William Cookworthy at Efford cemetery, PWDRO

31. Collier, William. Portrait of a Young Quaker: the early diary of John Collier 1790 – 91. Transactions of the Devonshire Association, vol 128. 1996. James, S A H. *The Church of Plymouth called Charles Church: the life continues.* Privately printed. 1964 ;Stephens, W.B. *Education in Britain 1750 – 1914.* Macmillan Press. 1998. A print showing the deck of a slave ship produced by the Plymouth Society for Effecting the Abolition of the Slave Trade in late 1788 found its way into the Friends House Library.

32. Collier, W., as above. A Jobation is a rebuke, usually long and tedious.

33. MM minutes 2nd month 1804 to 7th month 1804. Collier, W. as above.

34. Digest of births, marriages and burials, West Devon, in PWDRO; MM minutes 1st month 1821: in these minutes the overall numbers were increased by the births.

35. MM minutes 11th month 1807 to 3rd month 1808. Francis Knight in *A History of Sidcot School 1808 – 1908* (J.M. Dent.1908) mentions difficulty in getting subscriptions from Devon, but this is not altogether in line with what is in the Monthly Meeting minute book (see next chapter). His history gives no information on where pupils came from.

36. James, S A H. *The Church of Plymouth called Charles Church: the life continues.* Privately printed. 1964. For Mary Fox, Collier, W, as above. Several sources mention the school of industry at the end of the 18th century, in which the "Quaker ladies" were involved. W B Stephens (*Education in Britain 1750 – 1914.* Macmillan Press. 1998) has general information on Sunday schools and schools of industry.

37. Kingsbridge MM minutes 8th month 1785 and 10th month 1785 (three meetings within four days); Plymouth MM minutes 9th month and 10th month 1785; Devon QM minutes 10th month 1785; Plymouth Women's MM minutes 10th month 1785. The first Preparative Meeting minute book shows that most of the time they dealt with answering the Queries and appointing representatives to the Monthly Meeting.

38. Quarterly Meeting Sufferings book 1793 – 1828. The entry for 1796 is missing, but there exists a separate sheet for West Devon for that year. Yearly Meeting minutes 1796 note that some Friends are paying and direct Quarterly Meetings to see that Monthly Meetings "extend the necessary care". The Navy rate is explained in a printed briefing issued by Meeting for Sufferings explaining changes in the legislation.

39. Quarterly Meeting Sufferings book 1793 – 1828.

40. MM minutes 2nd month 1801 to 1st month 1802. Winfield, Rif. *British Warships in the Age of Sail*. Seaforth Publishing. 2007. The ship was broken up in 1808.

41. Kendall, J. *Memoirs of the Life and Religious Experience of John Kendall to which are added Letters . . . .* London. 1815.

42. Isichei, Elizabeth. *Victorian Quakers*. Oxford University Press. 1970

Notes on chapter 4: Philanthropy and evangelism 1800 to 1890

1. Census figures of 1801 and 1851. The *Devonport Estate Report* produced for the St Aubyn estate by a Mr Wingfield, 1841 (in PWDRO) says that local people attributed the loss of the opulent classes in Devonport to the uncertainty of the tenure imposed by the estate, but argues that the failure to match Plymouth in growth was primarily due to the decline of the dockyard. Information on sanitation and overcrowding from the *Report on the Sanitary Condition of Plymouth* by Rev W J Odgers, printed by Isaiah Keys, 1847.

2. Records of the special meeting and the re-building in a notebook in PWDRO. In the PM minutes 3rd month 1806, when the decision was eventually recorded, the original minute is amended to "It was there agreed on . . ."

3. P M minutes 5th month 1808. It was originally written as just nine pounds, and the 6/- was added above the line.

4. Prospectus in PWDRO. C W Bracken (*A History of the Plymouth Public School School.* Plymouth. 1927) lists the various names the school went under at different times.

5. Letters from Joseph Lancaster to Henry Woollcombe 1809 and 1810, in PWDRO

6. Plymouth Public Free School minute book in PWDRO

7. Wilcockson, R. *The Founding and History of the Society to 2012,* in *the Plymouth Athenaeum 1812 – 2012*, published by the Plymouth Athenaeum, 2012; Worth.

8. Press cutting and additional comment recorded in a brief notice in the Journal of the Friends Historical Society vol 17 no.1, 1920. There

are few newspapers available from this period, and the source has not been traced.

9. MM minutes 12th month 1812. The full testimony is given in an appendix.

10. Newcomers provision in PM minutes 12 month 1811. For Margaret Fox, Women's MM minutes 10th month 1815; identical wording in Men's MM minutes.

11. Joaquim José da Silva Maia. *Memorias historicas, politicas e filosoficas da Revolução do Porto*. Rio de Janeiro. 1841. Information from Toby Bainton. The statement in these memoirs that the Quakers were the only ones to help does not seem to be borne out by the contemporary reports in the Exeter and Plymouth Gazette. As usual, there is no mention in Quaker minute books.

12. MM minutes 7th month 1808. Letter of Joseph Cookworthy 24 July 1828 in disputes records in PWDRO; his dating of the letter is not in a Quaker manner, and when he died in 1833, although he was buried in the burial ground, he was marked as a non-member. There was a committee to decide on the burial of non-Quakers in the fairly small area. At the Quarterly Meeting (QM minutes 9th month 1828), it was decided not to pursue the matter (he was 74 at the time). Later in the century, an inappropriate gravestone for Thomas Were Fox was removed (MM minutes 7th month 1860). The information about the Norley Lane properties comes from a note at the back of the PM minute book 1791 – 1853, a letter tucked into the same minute book, and a minute, both of 1839, and PM minutes 9th month 1854.

13. MM minutes 12th month 1828

14. Beaver, Patrick. *The Match Makers*. Henry Melland. 1985; Milligan, Edward H. *Biographical Dictionary of British Quakers in Commerce and Industry 1775 – 1920* . Sessions Book Trust. 2007; list of members

1837 – 1936 in PWDRO. On 30 October 1850, the *Western Courier* reported that on the 23rd, Bryant & Burnell's soap factory in Coxside had burnt down, but the adjoining starch factory and house of Edward James were unaffected.

15. Henry Woollcombe's diary in PWDRO. C.A. Lewis *The Education of the Adult in Plymouth (1808 – 1941)*. PhD Thesis, University of Exeter. 1980.

16. Friends First Day Adult School minute book 1906 – 1912 in PWDRO; MM minutes 2nd month 1871; Adult School and Junior School papers in PWDRO. As often happened, Charlotte M James was given the same first name as her mother with a distinguishing middle name, Mary. The testimony is in MM minutes 3rd month 1915, and describes her as "of a retiring disposition".

17. Dymond, and PM minutes 9th & 11th month 1874, 9th month 1887, and 6th month 1888; property documents 1871 – 1928 in PWDRO. In 1871 it had been agreed to give up some land in the burial ground for the widening of Vennel Street, in return for land in Charles Street. Dymond remarked that he believed that part of the large grave for burying the bones removed from the burial ground at the Hoe now lay under the pavement in Vennel Street. The paying off of the mortgage was largely due to a donation of £400 from Charles Prideaux.

18. MM minutes 3rd month 1874

19. MM minutes 8th month 1875. Property papers in PWDRO. Friends Circulating Tract Association minutes in PWDRO: the records fade away after 1882, and maybe the Tract Association did too.

20. Testimony to Alfred P Balkwill MM minutes 7th month 1914; PM minutes 11th and 12th month 1870; Adult and Junior School papers

21. QM minutes; for the figures, 4th month 1874; membership list 1837 – 1936, counting the 19th century Plymouth members only. There were 32 Friends with their own business, typically merchants and chemists, and there were 16 employed, including clerks, salesmen and warehousemen

22. QM minutes 7th & 9th month 1875, and 1st month 1876. Not all Friends approved of the Quarterly Meeting date being changed without consultation, and it was minuted that it was not to be a precedent. *Western Morning News* various dates in September. No mention (apart from the paid announcements) in *Western Daily Chronicle* or the weekly *Devonport Independent & Plymouth & Stonehouse Gazette*. The press seemed much more interested in Cambridge University's extension work which was starting in Plymouth at the same time.

23. Dymond; PM minutes 10th month 1875, 3rd month 1882, 3rd & 6th month 1884; paper prepared by another Dymond, Robert, for the opening, in PWDRO. No press mention traced.

24. Typescript in premises records in PWDRO, reproduced in *Quakers at Swarthmore* booklet, ed, Rorie Smith, Chris Cabot and Sylvia Russell, 2003. C.R. Fox had resigned in February 1913. His name is recorded on a 1955 foundation stone of the Plymouth and South Devon Trustee Savings Bank as the Senior Trustee and chairman of the committee of management.

25. Photocopy of handwritten document sent to Plymouth Meeting by Heather Bailey of Bedford Meeting. It was written by her great-grandfather. C R Fox names Harriette Richardson as the last woman to wear a Quaker bonnet in Plymouth.

26. MM minutes 3rd & 4th months 1883

27. For Charles Prideaux, banker, clerk of the Monthly Meeting and a Minister, see Milligan, Edward H. *Biographical Dictionary of British Quakers in Commerce and Industry 1775 – 1920* . Sessions Book Trust. 2007. For Helen Balkwill (later Harris) and Alfred P Balkwill, see MM minutes 11th month 1879, 11th & 12th months 1880, 2nd & 12th months 1881. MM Ministry & Oversight minutes 3rd month 1881. J Rendel Harris in Oxford Dictionary of National Biography.

28. William Taylor, MM minutes 12th month 1876 & 2nd month 1877; Gustave & Elise Michaud, MM minutes 6th month 1887; Overseers minutes 1888 – 1909 passim.

29. Correspondence 1880 – 1911 in PWDRO; MM minutes 1st & 3rd month 1890; Overseers' minutes 1st month 1890. Home Missioners were Quaker evangelists, usually young, appointed in rural areas, and for some Friends they were too much like a paid ministry (Isichei, Elizabeth. *Victorian Quakers.* Oxford University Press. 1970). Thomas Litten denied that he had applied for the post of Home Missioner, and said he had been approached about it.

30. PM minutes 9th month 1881; MM minutes 5th month 1895, and 11th month 1897.

31. e.g. MM minutes 12th month 1890

32. Pen and Pencil Society minute book 1886 – 1898 in PWDRO; bound volume of contributions to the Society in the possession of PWDRO.

33. Western Morning News 1 November 1909; Annual Monitor; testimony in MM minutes. The Deputy Mayor was said to be speaking impromptu at the Sunday evening service for the people at the Guildhall, the day after Bray's death. The account of his remarks given in a funeral address by H Vigurs Harris (information on Individuals in PWDRO) is slightly different.

34. Sarah Fox, MM minutes 3rd month 1854; Elizabeth Prideaux (daughter of the first Sarah Abbott), 3rd month 1857; testimony to Sarah Anne Budge 3rd month 1905 – list of members for her arrival date.

Notes on chapter 5: World wars and Swarthmore Institute

1. MM minutes 2nd month & 8th month 1896; QM minutes 10th month 1896. When a committee was appointed to provide for Friends attending the Quarterly Meeting in Plymouth, its members were all women.

2. Special PM minutes 5th month & 8th month 1896. The plan in PWDRO shows that originally there were two ground floor rooms and a hall. The wall between the rooms was taken out, one doorway blocked up, two windows and three tube ventilators added. A platform with fixed bench and table was installed at the far end. The two fireplaces remained. The total length of the meeting room was about 27 feet, and because the original rooms were of different sizes, the width narrowed down from about 16 feet to about 14 feet. The benches and the number they seated were marked on the plan.

3. MM minutes 11th & 8th month 1904

4. PM minutes 11th &12th months 1896, 12th month 1897

5. Minute book of Treville Street Evening Meeting committee in PWDRO, passim

6. Ministry & Oversight meeting 3rd month 1896; MM minutes 6th & 8th month 1896, 6th & 12th month 1898, 3rd month 1899, 11th month 1900, 5th month 1901.

7. MM minutes 2nd month 1905. The *Western Morning News* mentioned

the meeting in its editorialising but did not report it.

8. Adult School minute book 1906 – 1912; MM minutes 12th month 1905. The outings included a steamer trip, and there were other social activities.

9. Overseers minutes 12th month 1918

10. Oxford Dictionary of National Biography; *Western Morning News* and *Western Daily Mercury* 11 to 15 April 1914. J Rendel Harris was a constant visitor to Plymouth Meeting, which even wrote a short testimony about him when he died in 1941 He was the brother of (Henry) Vigurs Harris, who had carried on his father's trade as a house decorator, was another convert to Quakerism, and became a leading local Friend, and happened to be the clerk of the Quarterly Meeting extension committee. Vigurs was a Liberal councillor and much involved in local charitable activity. *(Western Morning News* 13 December 1944)

11. MM minutes 8th to 11th month 1914; 12th month 1915. Charlotte M James, one of the Friends who volunteered, died in February 1915. Ralph Eliott, who had earlier declined the post of assistant clerk on the grounds of poor health, brought the concern about German and Austrian nationals to the Meeting and seems to have done most of the work.

12. Rubinstein, David. *Friends and War 1899 – 1945.* Journal of the Friends Historical Society vol 65, 2014 (published 2016). MM minutes 2nd month 1916. The MM minute book for 1897 to 1915 holds at the back some photos of Plymouth Friends. Most of these are of revered members in ripe age, but two are of young men, E Bonvile Fox (later Monthly Meeting clerk) and Leonard Harris, both in FAU uniform, and one is of Ernest Collins in RAMC uniform. The membership records show that all survived the war.

103

13. Hoare, Richard J. *John Hoare: A Pacifist's Progress*. Sessions Book Trust. 1998 (p 121). MM minutes 5th and 6th months 1917; Princetown Allowed Meeting minute book in PWDRO. Overseers' minutes say that many of the new attenders at the Princetown Meeting had come under Friends' influence while in Wormwood Scrubs.

14. MM minutes 9th month 1916; Building Committee minutes 1916 – 1920 in PWDRO; property papers in PWDRO; Religious Instruction committee minutes 2nd & 3rd months 1918. The building committee had originally said that the purchase price should not exceed £2500. One of the reasons for acquiring 76 & 78 was that it enabled the restrictive covenants on 72 to be extinguished, so increasing its value. It was sold to the Plymouth and South Devon Savings Bank. In September 1923 it was agreed that all property should be transferred to the Quarterly Meeting's trustees.

15. Overseers' minutes 12th month 1918

16. Overseers minutes; M M minutes (for C A Goodbody, 2nd month 1939). G Rendel Harris was the son of H Vigurs Harris.

17. The invitation to the opening (among papers at PWDRO) actually says "master words of English literature", but this seems to be a misprint in an invitation printed in haste for an event the following week. Other information from article *The Plymouth Experiment* in the Quaker periodical *Workers at Home and Abroad* March 1921. Extension committee minutes are missing.

18. Overseers' minutes; M M minutes. Information on the Ridges comes from *Leighton Park: a history of the school*, by S W Brown, privately published in 1952. Surviving records say nothing about formally adopting the name Swarthmore.

19. Swarthmore seems to have been called Swarthmore settlement, Swarthmore institute or Swarthmore adult education centre, at whim.

The earlier formal documents name it as Swarthmore Settlement, but the name on the gable end in 1921 was Swarthmore Institute. Council minutes and annual reports exist from the 1926/27 session.

20. New building committee minutes 1924 – 1926; appeal document 1924; plans as approved by the Borough council 1924 and also as existing in 1936, in PWDRO; photograph in *The Plymouth Experiment* in *Workers at Home and Abroad* March 1921.

21. Information from tabular statements available from 1922; Finance Committee minutes 1930 and 1970.

22. Letter and minute in "activities" papers in PWDRO. The party included the daughter of John and Blanche Ridges, Joan Ridges, who was at some point the secretary of the Young Friends central committee and was soon to marry Francis Lawson. (Robinson, C. *Lawsons: The Story of a Family Business since 1904*. Plymouth. 2016*)*.

23. Papers on allotments for the unemployed, apparently Astor family records, in PWDRO; MM minutes 12th month 1931.

24. Papers on allotments for the unemployed, in PWDRO; *Western Morning News* 12 Jan 1933.

25. Swarthmore annual reports. The two lecturers were Messrs Mann and Gunningham, the latter being the Ministry of Agriculture adviser (information from John Lawson).

26. MM minutes; plans and appeal documents in PWDRO. The appeal document did not mention the remodelling at the southern end of the building.

27. Minute book of the Refugee Committee 1938 – 1942 and report 1942 (courtesy of John Lawson)

28. MM minutes 11th & 12th months 1940. The WFCC minutes show that Janet Harris had already been a president, and that at the time Frances Absalom was secretary of their hostel committee.

29. The minute arose from a concern of Arthur Gage, who drafted it. (Dr) Norah Goodbody was the clerk at the time. The businesses whose premises were destroyed were: C A & W Goodbody, confectioners and caterers; Harris & Sons, decorators and fine art dealers; Fox Eliott & Co, timber merchants; Fox Roy & Co, shipping agents; Bond Pearce & Eliott, solicitors; F T B Lawson, tool merchants; Owen & Sons, bakers & confectioners; the city premises of Alfred N Balkwill, dentist. (MM minutes, especially 5th month 1946; printed minute and reports on the two hostels in PWDRO.

30. MM minutes 12th month 1945 to 11th month 1946, and 11th month 1947. A postcard of Mutley Plain at this time captions it as Plymouth's shopping centre.

31. Donald Bentley joined Friends in 1948, about the same time that he was appointed assistant warden of Swarthmore. The Gages formally resigned as wardens in September 1948 and moved to Croydon, where he died soon afterwards. (List of members in PWDRO). Prison ministers mentioned in MM minutes November 1954 & August 1956

32. MM minutes July & Dec (special) 1955 & June 1963; papers & press cuttings relating to Cookworthy reburial in PWDRO.

33. MM minutes August 1954 & April 1960; booklet *Quakers at Swarthmore* (see above), particularly the contributions by Joan Fox, Irene Curtis and Rex Crouch; numbers attending MM noted for a time from 1955 to 1957.

Glossary

Church: in Quaker usage, the body of Friends.

Convincement: the Quaker equivalent of conversion; the process by which those attending Quaker meetings became members.

Days of the week: see the explanation at the beginning of the Notes.

Discipline: see under Meeting.

Disownment: the practice of declaring someone to be out of unity or no longer in membership of the Society.

Distraint: the seizure of goods and chattels to meet a debt, or pay a fine. In Quaker history, most often used in relation to the payment of ecclesiastical rates and tithes.

Elders have a responsibility for the right conduct of the meeting for worship, and for spiritual nurture. Their function was originally to give guidance and support to new Ministers (see below).

Evangelicalism in Christianity is characterised by an insistence on the need to accept Jesus as a personal saviour, usually through a conversion experience.

Friend and Quaker are used interchangeably.

Leat: artificial watercourse, used for providing a water supply or for providing water power, or both.

Meeting In the text, Meeting with a capital refers to the organisation; meeting in lower case refers to the event, usually the meeting for worship. **Yearly Meetings** are the ultimate authorities in independent units of the Society of Friends. **Meeting for Sufferings**, originally a body formed to take action on sufferings, came to be the authority in between Yearly Meetings. **Quarterly Meetings** were the main decision-making body over a considerable area, often a county, for most of the period covered by this history. **Monthly Meetings** were subject to Quarterly Meetings and had responsibility for membership, discipline, and the care of members. All these may be referred to as "Meetings for discipline", that is, for good church order. **Preparative Meetings** originally met to do some of the preparatory work for Monthly Meetings, where these had more than one Quaker Meeting within them. Plymouth had the peculiarity that the Preparative Meeting was used for property transactions. All Meetings for discipline originally had restricted membership and until 1896 were divided into men's and women's meetings, which had separate functions. Practice changed before formal changes were made. (Unless the women's meeting is specified, the mention of a meeting for discipline before 1896 refers to the men's meeting.)

Minister: Although they did not have a paid clergy, and anyone could speak or pray in Meeting for Worship, for their first three centuries British Quakers recognised certain members as having particular gifts in preaching, and they were recorded as ministers and would sit on the bench for ministers and elders facing everyone else in the meeting for worship. When recorded ministers travelled in the ministry outside their Monthly Meetings, they would be given a travelling minute, usually endorsed by the meetings they had visited.

Months: see the explanation at the beginning of the Notes.

Overseers: the office of overseer was brought in towards the end of the 18th century, and has a responsibility for the care of members. They took over some functions from the Women's Meeting. For most of the time covered by this history, it was not uncommon for a Friend to be appointed as both elder and overseer, appearing on both lists.

Presbyterianism was characterised by a system of church government without bishops, and emphasis on preaching by qualified and ordained ministers.

Queries were formal questions which subordinate Meetings were required to answer. They varied over time, and later became designed for personal use.

Steeplehouse: the Quaker term for a church building.

Testimony can mean (a) an act or practice based on religious conviction, such as refusing to fight or take oaths; or (b) a statement about the life of a deceased Friend, written for the edification of others; or (c), in older usage, a statement of faith.

Truth usually refers to the special insights which Quakers believed they had.

Index